The Journey of Uncovery

Abiyah Reinha Alexanda de Carvalho

authorHOUSE

AuthorHouse™ UK
1663 Liberty Drive
Bloomington, IN 47403 USA
www.authorhouse.co.uk
Phone: UK TFN: 0800 0148641 (Toll Free inside the UK)
       UK Local: (02) 0369 56322 (+44 20 3695 6322 from outside the UK)

Published by AuthorHouse 04/18/2022

ISBN: 978-1-5049-9979-3 (sc)
ISBN: 978-1-5049-9980-9 (e)

Kirkus Review-

Debut author de Carvalho offers a semiautobiographical novel about a young woman's perilous journey from Africa to Europe. readers will find that navigating the prose can prove challenging, as some passages are awkwardly phrased, including this description of life in England: "For many years since the family eloped to the UK seeking political asylum my father did not work, actually since he escaped from my country even when; good jobs opportunity came his way he shattered it and chose to live off benefits." The challenges of the text are not without pleasures, though, such as when a horrible smell is described as being "as loud as a Lion roaring wild noise." The book is enlivened with smatterings of Portuguese, and although the convergence of languages isn't seamless, the authentic feel of the work is beyond question. It's an undeniably personal, if unpolished, account of the refugee experience that takes readers to places they won't expect to go.

Pacific Book Review-

author Abiyah de Carvalho recalls her early childhood in Angola. Her mother, a beautiful, gracious woman, did her best to raise the girl, called "Lucianna" in this account. Lucianna had an older brother, Lelo, who sometimes seemed to live more freely than she or her mother, but even he was once savagely beaten by their father for nothing more than playing among his friends with a water gun. Lucianna, scarred by such events, grew up feeling herself to be more perceptive than those around her. She was highly sensitive to the evil done by her father, whom she describes as a "domestic terrorist," referring to his violence in their home. She came to believe that her father was a practitioner of witchcraft, still common in many parts of Africa 'at the closing of their European life residing country'; When Lucianna was about nine, her mother fled with all her children and, assisted by relatives, flew to Paris.

"...our lives..like a discovery channel. Whatever; is done in the dark does not remain in the dark; GOD brings it to light."

This memoir by an Angolan-born author is both warm and sad. Lucianna (fictional name) is the daughter of parents whose life values were polar opposites due to very different backgrounds. During the civil war in Angola, Lucianna's family fled to Paris when she was nine.

'And Her father's who has now passed away reputation for military service while; a danger to the family's survival also helped them escape. Highly respected among relatives, friends, also loved by his community for his good deeds to them and country respectably so according to his army credentials which played the tagged.'

But his family knew a darker side of him. He ruled the house with an iron will.

About the Book

A, real life story of a young person who saw and lived the moments which; are recorded in writings in this book. Motivated and, influence by; how many ethnic background family live in their household going through the days of their lives in silent suffering like hers. Those; who both live within the borders of Europe, as refugees statutes or full time residents and thought that on arriving in Europe their family life was also, going to change just as their global location had change. This; happens often after believing in a false reality displayed by a spouse, usually by husbands.

Unfortunately;

Many fall short of remembrance of who they are and where they come from. They forget that GOD who had delivered them from the oppression they faced in their homeland and brought them to their dreamland for greater opportunities; is He who will continue to deliver them from bondage and repression.

The; real life story written in this piece is a testimony of His hand at work.

GOD does exist and He is truly awesome. This; is a story that many people avoid telling but; is how and what many go through.

An insight of the unseen reality.

From 1994 to this current age of great economic obstacles, entertainment destruction, and uncertainty settled on the face of a supposed great and bright future for people of all nations. Luciana had no idea of the challenges she was to face and is facing in her lifetime as; she consciously stands in limbo between her birth soil homeland and; the foreign soil homeland where Luciana grew up in for the thirteen years of her life and where she is forever a stranger. A stranger, Luciana is by race, culture, and a not understood class and standards by her uniqueness. However she is marked by every place and everything she has been through. Her life carries a mark of everything.

Of the; most recent development of Luciana's life, her studies had always taken the biggest space in her life, occupying her mind, brain, and heart with art. Whilst; most young people of her age and adults found refuge in destructive paths of entertainment; and living a life of fornication, and sexual immorality; her education was her most precious refuge. She held on to her studies as though it was her only true friend 'GOD gifted her with. The educational access; that many don't have; she has, talent and love for her talent; 'striving for a happy future'; is the way she looked at it. Just like when; the young 9 years old girl before escaping her country with her mother and mano Lelo of ten years of age at the time, who she often called him only by Lelo, and two little brothers of the age of months old babies. The war in her country, with the Angolan people viciously killing

1

each other rather it was in a battle field frontline, an individual being attacked on the street at night during a quiet promenade by a gang of bandits, or a neighbour going against the other neighbour because of unpaid debt but more common causes were the clash of opposition supporters of political and military parties. Many Angolans fled the country leaving their homes to find refuge in the European country of Portugal; many of the Angolan nationals who left the homeland also, changed their nationality and identity completely to erase the traces of where they come from 'Angola'. Out of shame; shame and dislike of the war in Angola; Luciana grew up as a child who could had have it all, a good life with privileges but of imprisonment, in a healthy and wealthy household with both parents though the relationship between Julianna and papa was not always smooth and happy for Julianna, but it was not totally uncomfortable for them. Her mother had a certain financial independence that allowed her to be able to improvise for Lucianna and her siblings in food, clothes, toys, sweets, pocket money to take to school although as children; they never really held money for themselves unless if they were to be out of Julianna's sight to go to a barrack to buy sweets and biscuits. Even at that they were never seen out in public, or as often. People knew her and of Lucianna, and her siblings but she knew not them with; no child friends in the neighbourhood to play with. She was not allowed to play out; her father's orders they were. Except from family friends children who came around and she with her family went to visit in their homes, at least twice or three time a year.

The small world; I grew up in and deprived of social development for the most part of it. Everyone was not good enough to come close to my family even, including most relatives, but many of them did not come by not because; maybe they were not good enough. It was because; they were just not interested. In other words 'No love and care'; especially that mother is not like them or from where they are from. The Angolan stigma against Congolese people from Zaire, especially the woman; they said that 'they are witches, ugly, trashes they ate people...' a Zaire Congolese would be alienated, and despised. There was also a mind myth that my mum was stealing my dad's money just because she is from Zaire, and to his family she had to go.

Interested to know, be close and love us. My mother was the envy of many women from her husband's family and a few in her own family not because; her husband was a FAA official for the woman in my father's family but; she was different as to the other woman in that family and still is. In; values, elegance, very well mannered, intelligent, unique and beautiful and a different mindset. She saw other woman to be woman with potential to excel, and disposing herself to help those who wanted her help when it was needed if asked for it, and not a competition. Comparing to the women in my father's side of the family... Both housewives, working wives, aunties, nieces, sisters in law, sisters and cousins many were very classless, and they ported themselves with no elegance no general regards for appearance presentation. Charm is no found in their character and personality. 'Smirking'; I always found it to be amusing and sad that; people do a at times multiple copy cut of your image a goal for them to achieve, with the focus of competing against you... Their target has shifted from my mother to me, now their daughters silently display their declarations of visual competition. Wanting to know my wear about, my stage in life, what I do and how I do of 'personal details of my life'; and what is going to be my next hair style, what or how do I put together my outfits; and the next thing thrown at my face is that; I have now become a goal for imitation of my personality, character, style and fashion what ever they feel will score me. When they don't get it right; they get irritated and jealous 'They can cry too for all I care'.

A trend of overweight woman goes on around the city capital of my country; whereas money is flashed out in the air, for a whisper 'she has a good life'; but yet she lives less then the quality of life; and a lying snare settled down in them, and yet they see and find nothing wrong with them. Some proclaim that Jesus Christ is Lord, but their way of living is a lie, only the walls of their houses truly knows what their lives are like; not that ones private life should be a public discussion, but; why must an individual make someone else life a public discussion?

Their close relative knows them and even so; a fake life and image is also managed for display, and as somebody not close to her she will only approach you to know you, but to imitate you away from your presence to the rest of the family and relatives which; you don't know or saw once in your life therefore; they are strangers to you. You may say. Theft of identity, and your personal life a joke to them, and the story for gossip. My father's family... But; I have been in worst situations, where I was robed of immensely huge amount of money, and material good, I was robed off of my chance for a good and better life, and furthering my education to where I wanted to achieve in life. The thieves; did with pleasure, and a gang located in London and all over the world moving around the globe to look for a chance in life to steal from others, if they have to murder you they will just that; they may have possession of what is yours. They live in hideouts; in companies and they enrich other people using what belongs to you, without your consent. Their word means nothing to them. They lie about their age, name, address, place of work, they will say that they work for well reputed companies meanwhile they own criminal legalised illegal companies for their criminal organization. Their mothers; are part of it and, a thing that runs in their family it is. They are; the sponsors of crime, the instigators of crime in our cities, some do it because it is part of their pact with the devil, in exchange for riches, influence not so much of fame except if is for their personal career goal. They are the same people who divert the course of justice in the law. They bow their knees to satan and hide behind religion and say that; they worship and love GOD, they will join you in prayer for a good cause but; behind your back, they will fight against you as their master satan is your enemy and the enemy of life. But some of them who, stand strong for their lord in satan, don't even dream to enter a bible believing church, or pray to GOD especially not in the name of Jesus, and when they do it, they do it in fear their God satan, their lord satan and their demons beats them up at night in their next meeting, they get punishments and have to redeem themselves with blood sacrifices to please satan. 'Why are people killing people?'; used to ask myself I knew it was the work of the devil, but did not have the intelligence and wisdom to understand the mind of satanic conspiracy and the redemption of blood sacrifice. Power! By climbing over the gazillion dead bodies. They lay lives low down to satan for it. Millions strive for the power, money and fame, but many fell short to realise that in Jesus Christ there is life, light, and peace therefore; power, fame and riches is free.

One of the most dangerous gang in the world, and each person in it is an underdog. They call themselves 'The rich gang'; drinking off the wine reserved for the truest children of the destiny, the children of GOD. They should have never forgotten that it was David who defeated Goliath by GOD for the children of Israel, and not the other way around. True identity of theirs is of old age they are, they deny their children and their children say they have no father and mother or, one of the other; just that they can fool you, then take pleasure in destroying your life. Their mothers are; behind them clapping and cheering for their criminal hypocrite and delinquent sons and daughters. Children of satan with pride they are, they have no head, legs, and arms; but an empty life they are.

"'Cuidado, muito cuidado com essa familia do voço pai, mhm. Não prestão, melhore estudar a pessoa e põe na oração antes de confiar!'"

My mother always says; but without condemnation to anyone in particular, and she is not wrong; she knows the character of the individuals she met in Angola where my father devised against her; I do not think I was born then, however Lelo was... the plot was first for Lelo and my mother, but as, the family grew it extended against the rest of us. It was; a plot planned and strategized by him, that man, my dad; the name of the plot is witchcraft; my mother accidently stepped on it by, walking on it without knowing that her husband is an antichrist, a devil man, and that he had brought his village witchcraft lifestyle in their home, and worst to kill, destroy and steal from her and, her son. Nevertheless... And the people she met in my father's birthplace, and here. By far; she prefers the one she knows and have always been close to her since her arrival in Angola; "I too, prefer the ones I was close to in my child hood"; them I have always known to be my only relatives and friends, from my father's side. They were there but also our personal space was respected, and the sense of good family and friendship, and trust to a certain degree too. More then the relatives who emerged into our lives when I was a little bit older in the age of young adolescence, who I know nothing about; their where about they were never seen anywhere when I was a child but; yet they have come to reap something for themselves out of my life, our lives, some relatives that I did not know and I now know have normal understandable reason. Is always good to chase your dreams, the circumstances of life. An insight they want and pretend to be what they are not, but this character I have also seen in few members of my mother's family, and there is a specific one. She also was not there in my growing up years, nor was she there; when my mother needed someone closest to her. She is directly very close in relations to my mother.

A place I grew up, a place I miss, a place my heart longs to go back to one day, and the place that has changed immensely far from my sight, that I was not there to see the changes. A country that was once a war place for its, citizens, is now giving a second chance at well being to the advanced in age; giving great opportunities to its nation especially the young people, at least is what I hear these days from Ursula. My friend who has now been going back and forth from Luanda to London;

I also hear the same from my cousins during their telephone conversations with my father, and when they come to our house from Luanda, Angola. It's funny, because he is not there but; he insists that nothing has changed in Luanda, and if it has; it has only been reformed to worst. Can he be right? According, to his diplomatic analysis, plus conclusions and instincts as a man who has served the FAA (Forças Armada Angolana) he was not a soldier who fought in the war battlefield. Oh no! He was an official his grade was Tenant coronel or higher; I cannot remember well 'woo it has been long since I last remember seeing him I his army training or official uniform'; which I also know that he will never be seen in it again. He carried a three or four stars on his shoulders attached to his uniforms, which he wore every day. Back then, I was a daddy's little girl and I often thought he was the most powerful man in the world, out casting all the American presidents, and Russian rulers too. I looked up to him and extremely proud I was; of him. Comparing to today, at the stares of my discoveries, in regard to this man who I call dad with no other option left, but to call him so. Some friends who no longer have their father or never had one, better known their father, know have had the privilege of knowing how my father is; the story of my family; however today some of these same so called friends are also the ones who discredit the purity and honesty of the true stories of my life, and its content of life. The experiences, the evidences, the fights, the long sad faces, tears, frustration, the lack of peace, joy and trust; they now discredit all because Malto is alive and not dead, therefore; I should be happy and understanding of him... apparently!

I was the closest to him; and able to study and find out about his truest character much sooner then my siblings, I understood things earlier then all the others; with an eye for details and understanding what others cannot understand. Speaking of what others do not understand nor can they speak off, and uncovering the very hidden but; unhidden skin layer. Details make all the difference and have always made the difference.

Beneath The Beautiful
and Perfect Surface

"Mãmã! Papa foi aondé?" I often used to ask my mother, and she always would say "'Foi resolver um problema'"; sometimes she used to reply saying "I don't know Lucianna"; as my dad never used to tell her his affairs outside the house nor take her out either to fancy places and dates. And anything official or important information about what her husband was doing outside the house she found out, she used to find out on her own, by her own means. The times that he took my mother out was on family outing very few occasions, and I remember one time when he told us that he was taking us to the city at Marginal, Luanda; it was around the midevening time. It was nine in the even when he took us to Wimpy, only because we overly begged to eat burger; that night would have been our first time to eat burger made in a restaurant or street, when we entered Wimpy; we followed his lead to our table. I felt disappointed; we all thought that we each were going to have a burger meal, but instead he ordered ice cream for each one of us and for himself he ordered a double sized burger meal, which include chips and drink. Lelo wanted a burger too alike me, my mum, and aunty; my mother's little sister; we had asked for it however; he kept on cancelling our order of burger as we were making them to the waitress right there at the table in front of us. "Mãmã eu queiro um amburg (Mother I want a burger). Fala no papa! (Tell father!)"; I mourned to my mother over and over again; but he could hear me very clearly, and he said:

"Is too expensive"; then said that I was too young to eat a burger, and then he said take your ice cream or I will never bring you out again. "Take it fast is late, we have to go home now"; he was without patience and contended a zero tolerance attitude as usual, as if it was a burden to spend time with us... His family.

It would have actually been better if we had stayed at home without; him around of course; we would have kept ourselves busily entertained and free to do as we pleased as long as; Lelo and I were behaving well as usual not jumping on the sofa, screaming or swearing and playing on or with the wall which; we never did any of those. Our neighbours always thought of us as being very different and special children and; highly educated and disciplined. We were very clean too, and posh; we spoke well with clean grammar and well mannered and people disbelieved that there were children who were born and being raised in our household. Just like; when they saw my mother they did not think she was also a mother, as she always looked stunning, and had a beautiful body; her frame, composure etc. she had a great body and she was very classy and elegant.

My father was unfair, mean, rude, and disrespectful to my mother though, including to his childhood friends, employees, although he never really did give any attention to his employees at work or outside of work related topics, and discussions. As far as the maids; and nannies who worked for us my mother took care of them and their needs and their wages were received directly from my mother to them. Leaving the guards to my father to deal with. I often noticed these attributes of a proud man in my dad from the type of hospitality and treatment he used to offer to his guests at home in Luanda, I could already see the man he really is, but what could a daddy's girl could really have done? Plus; I was just a child and I did not understand many things. Luciana, waved it all off to the back of her head. All I knew was that I loved my father so much and he loved me too. We were close like a finger its nail, a very strong bond, and stronger bond then the one I had with my mother and everybody with close relations to the family knew of my unbreakable bond with my father. The latest, I had seen my dad throwing shades of pride was to a close long time friend of his; it was in our home in Forestdale, when Ankle Abel came to London for the first time to visit us and reunite with my dad as old friends and far apart cousins who grew up together but; have not met in a long time. He had come from Poland, with also the agenda to find work in the UK, as things were very difficult in Poland his former hometown.

Friars Wood is a cursed home. 'I feel sick, sadness, anger, deep disappointment in just remembering of the time we lived in 143'

143, is the house where the most part of my growing up had happened. The house in which; I began to see life, and my father for their truest colours, the house I started to understand things as they have always been. My dad in ugliness, arrogance which brought bitterness, deep sadness, desperation for a better kind of life amongst one another as a family, in our hearts, mind and soul. Except, from my dad; he seemed to never want to see us and other people happy or see himself in better conditions for the family sake. He has his private if not privates bank accounts outside of the country, which contains millions from the businesses my mother started that he took over without giving a word nor allowing a word of defence from my mum for her businesses. Where he hides his money, only his family have access to it, but I don know if they also have their free way to take money... But I in many occasion they have had this freedom.

Ever so controlling; controlling the benefits money even the milk voucher.

That house was the house that brought my mother to realisation that she had indeed married and stuck along aside a very undeserving man. A domestic terrorist. Although, it had taken her many years for her to finally begin to open her eyes, and become wise as a woman and a mother and own her role of a parent 'protector'; just a protector. While it took my mãmã all these years to wise up about; the person she is married to for many years, I on the other hand watched how life was on the daily base and learned how things were in my family as I took on each new day at a time. Quiet, obedient, gracious, hurt and refused to be hurt and become a victim; I also had my own strong character and will which; I never lost. I knew who I was, what I wanted, where I wanted to go in life and who I wanted to become. 'Identifying myself to be a wise and righteous women of my future'; is one of the things of what I wanted.

143 Friars Wood; is not just the place that my mother opened her eyes to the reality that her family and children have been suffering from, but it brought pain, exhaustion, and deep suffering... As though she was imprisoned tide up and squashed into a glass bottle then thrown into the dark pit, along with her four birth children; all thrown into the dark pit; and were it hit against the rocks along the way. The pit that was dug for us, and a plot against us. But I could not see the reason why it was done so.

Lucianna never saw a tear drop from her mother's eyes, except from the time her father physically attacked her mother and hit her in the face because she spoke the truth about his family; his father mainly, the witchcraft practices and senses occult that my father never spoke of about his father's way, which Malto is also very much a part of. But; instead he used to insult my mother and her father saying that he is a wizard and his money was made from blood sacrifices, which is untrue. I saw this as an example of his paranoia; he blames others to cover up his and his family mess, his parents, siblings, and grand parents, his gods of darkness, his cousins and nieces as well as; nephews including his daughter the one; which my mother adopted.

Ohm. He has no physical evidence that connected to the spiritual realm that shows or implies his accusations are true; meanwhile his father had a long physical proof of truck record that prove him to be so. He had done it before, but amid all the problems they had gone through as a family and were still united. Lucianna thought somewhere at that time her father was going to be a changed man; a better dad to her and her brothers, a better husband to her mother, and a better friend to his own friends even! However nooohoo. The redemption of a lower lifestyle did not humble him, and he thought that he was too good for anything and bigger then everybody he encountered was a vivid power of control in him.

In 143 Friars Wood; I saw my dad for the first time in his truest colour, and a huge disappointment I felt in my heart; my first love is not my first love, the mirror image of what I wanted my husband to be as I thought, and I do not want to get married to a man like him. I will not marry a man like my father. My mother calls 143 'á maldita casa'; what I learned, found out, and saw whilst living at that house was scary, I saw a fraction of darkness in its different shades and forms, but it didn't just end there, it followed me till today after my degree graduation.

When it came to Lelo! Malto My father always made sure, Lelo would be the odd one out, he would deeply hurt him, and saddened him with his gross, degrading, disrespectful, and offensive words of insults on a daily bases.

"'Seu Cabrão de merda!" "Vocé é um stupido, buro, macaquo!" "Seu feio"; "Buro sai d'aqui", "Vou tì partir à cara, bisho, seu inutil"'.

He looked down on Lelo everyday at the given moment, every day was an opportunity; he only needed the moments out of the days to take a look at his face to start bullying Lelo; for example:

The mornings were always questionable mornings as to why did Lelo had to endure all the mistreatments, child abuse, yes child abuse. Physical, verbal, emotional and mental psychological assaults and such a hardship from his father from the age of as little as one year of age. Of course; he had to endure it he was just a child unless someone took a stand for him; and that was his family and home, where else should he have gone to for peace and love? But mother could. Lelo is the eldest child of our parents, and with a father that has always treated him in an ill manner not wanting to be there for Lelo, in a positive manner, being there for Lelo to show and give him his fatherly love and attention, Malto is not an inspirational role model I see; maybe to the people of his birth village and town. Lelo lucked in male friendship at home; left feeling lonely as; there was not a male figure in his life that he could relate to his younger brothers were still too young to have the kinds of conversations a adolescent of his age would have been having, and still to look up to him too.

I remember a sunny hot afternoon summer around three o'clock, Lelo was playing water fight with the other neighbouring kids at the front of the house and running around the garages too, it seemed fun, the kids looked very happy, excited and enjoying themselves having fun. It was the perceived sensation of 'good times, and great times', as though they were having the time of their lives. Every kid had his and hers own multiple bright colours water gun, that; which called attention to each other and from one another, and me too... I wished to be outside playing with all the other kids; like my brother, but I was scared of what my mother would have said or thought of me at the time.

A law had just come out about fake guns and a pistol as well as; real guns, but that was a law for the criminals and gang member as; there were crimes of robbery with the use of deadly weapons to threat lives in order to rob people. Poor Lelo My father took that moment when Lelo was playing as another opportunity of the day against Lelo, twisting and twirling the moment to be something negative.

Life for Lelo looked happier, as he was playing and running around with the other kids outside then inside the house. I in the indoor knew that; what happened that afternoon was really going to happen. Inside the house was my mother, my father, my two younger brothers, and ankle Abel; who was a good ankle but not as angelic as the angel Gabriel; but he helped us a lot, and he was the father figure we longed for especially to Lelo; we managed to feel lighter and unburdened like how children are supposed to be and feel especially; in certain disturbing and sad situation my father put my mother through and especially Lelo. My little stepsister was outside too running around after the bigger kids and trying to get involved in the water fight summer season game of the year.

I was standing at the kitchen door after I did my turn of washing up the dishes of lunch, and my mother was in the kitchen, as always, preparing coffee to serve the visitor father's guest; my ankle Abel and my dad who were sitting at the living room watching the television as, the Olympic games were on. Sometimes straight after lunch, mother would start cooking dinner, I recall her to be more like an employee of hard labour and a slave to my dad. That's how much and hard; she was always working, as if it wasn't enough for her to bare all at home she was also working three different jobs.

All of a sadden my father started yelling at Lelo from inside the house, and talking rubbish about his person

"Olha a quele gajo, burro, não têm vergonha!? (Look at that dumb, shit of guy, he has no shame!?)"

"Ele vai lavar essa roupa? Ta brincar com aqua!? Caralhio. Sem vergonha a brincar como uma criança (Will he wash this clothe? He is playing with water "caralho". Playing like a child with no shame"

He then got up from his sit, rushed to the house main door, opened the door, called Lelo to him, and Lelo came close and said "yes dad"; and before he could finish saying dad, my dada

14

drugged him by his shirt, violently pulled him inside the reception entrance area not far at all from the door, and shuttered the door behind him with a strong kick making the noise '¡BOOOom!'; I heard Lelo saying "Fig ou que? (What have I done?)"; the total opposite of the fun that was happening outside the house was taking place at that very moment. My dad started battering Lelo with blows of punches as of a grown man who was fighting and blowing his fellow grown man. He kicked, punched, slapped, banged his head against the wall so hard that we all heard the sound of the heavy knock of Lelo's head against the wall three times 'BOOOM, BOOM, BOOM!'; then punched him again and kicked more whilst swearing at him at the same time saying "cabrão, burro, macaco, sua ova" "voçé, voçé es um burro, seu macaco"; and my ankle started saying to my dad to leave it alone, implying it was normal for kids of his age to play. He called my dad few times, but there was no answer from him and; no stopping of the battering, he was too busy and enjoying himself battering his son to bust up lips and other physical injuries, as if he was fighting his worst enemy who also was a big grown up man of his age and size. What a shame I thought to my self. Standing in the living room now, slowly approaching the reception entrance area with my heart sinking down to my stomach and thinking that's it; that's how he will kill Lelo. He will kill him.

I was scared, terrified, trembling, nervous, and tired; tired of the same day in and; day out pain the terrorism my father in frustrated on us all that; was and always seemed to be directed to Lelo. I wanted to go and pull my dad away from my brother, but I was scared at that point. Where I come from; you do not touch your parent not matter how wrong they are towards you, although I was not going to attack my dad, but I know, he was later on going to turn it to something else. And; in a scenario like that, to touch Malto or to try to separate that meant that you are disrespectful and inconsiderate to him, and an imbecile for trying to help Lelo, and he was will then also give you your portion of it. You will suffer the consequence of the good did against his oppression, condemned by his deed.

So scared. To find him struggling for his life in the hand of dad because of what was happening. But, at the same time I could not physically reach the reception area; I felt paralyzed physically, psychologically, and emotionally drained, scared for my brother, and my friend's life. I was so scared, and felt so unsafe; l started screaming at my mum in panic whilst I trembled of fear

"Olha, olha, olha! (Look, look, look!) go, go, stop him, tell him to stop, he will kill him, he will kill Lelo, he will kill him, he's beating him hard, can't you hear? Go Go, goo!"; she then after a while walked out of the kitchen and started saying to my dad "Malto para, já chega, chega Malto! (Malto stop, is enough, Malto enough!)"; he didn't stop till after forty five minutes to an hour of battering Lelo. I feared, but it was not the fear of great and at most respect for my dad no; it was the fear of terror and that I was maybe loosing my brother.

I was sad, and upset especially that, there were adults in the house who were witnessing the domestic violence and child abuse battering so close to them but no one of them did anything to save the kid, and the other seemed to be thinking 'its okay, it will stop soon', probably.

Relatively in accordance to the time it took her to start saying something and out of the kitchen, and the relaxation of the back then favourite uncle; Like; mother said "'Be careful with your father's family'"; they are always with hidden agendas including and, especially him my dad and his daughter and malicious plan B, C to Z, by now I already know and understand the thing going on around, as GOD is not dead or death, and I thank him for his protection. Mother has been seeing things of late; between her husband, his daughter, her sister and many other woman and so have I; you won't understand, but I do because GOD saves me, and is why I see what I see. They; are all the same, regardless

16

of the smiles they display with their faces. Hypocrites they are and, have always been.

Could not; just couldn't anymore, take it, see it, be in that house, in that family; my family. I felt so sorry for my brother, my mother, my three younger siblings and myself. That had deeply hurt me to see him hurt and hurting everyday, and unhappy, forcing a smile to hide his physical pain emotional and psychological abuse. Even; when he could not smile because he lucked strength, motif and meaning to smile. As, a kid he was not allowed to be a kid.

'But, dad never abused me like he did to Lelo, why?'; that soon became the reason and force why I distanced myself from Malto. I felt like as though; Lelo did let some of what happened to him in my dad's hand, because he wanted me know that he would come for me after he was done with him and while he took the abuse I should have prepared myself, or maybe find my self-defence place and to protect myself against my dad. But I was always self-defensive of myself against my dad during those years of my life, although; I was the closest to him.

Deep down and deep inside Lucianna's mind; she always thought 'my dad treats Lelo the way he does because; maybe Lelo has something in him that dad sees and want, but can't touch to take it away for his own use, and he is very jealous of Lelo. He wants to take from his son what he cannot take because; it was not gifted to him'; she was sure of that with a very suspicious mind about her father ways towards her brother.

Lelo then walks into the house, making his way up the stairs to his room, to wash himself and change his water socked and enlarged clothing, and I also, clocked that he was red and his face swollen too. I went into silence, and was sad. Lelo was around twelve or thirteen years old, and I was eleven or twelve years of age. Is it fair? Is this how life was meant to be? A three, four, six, eleven to twelve and a twelve to thirteen years old, living in so much violence and abuse, in the house they lived with both parents, in a country of law... Conviction overwhelmed me slowly but; abruptly gathered in my heart. Sometimes I was close to calling the police to take my dad away from our home; or even report at the school about what was happening at home. But I always had to remember that in my 'culture' a child must not go against hers or his parents, especially father no matter how wrong they are, and also God would not have been happy with me if I did such because; I always thought that it would lead us to a court judgement. As what mum used to tell me whenever; I told her I was going to call the police. My mother terrified with fear, she was always scared of him, I knew it and still know it, even when she denies it by saying as a parent there are things that should not be discussed in front of the children, and then she goes on saying "you think I don't say anything to him? I'm not scared of him! This is not subject for you. "Enough!"; But I still knew she was scared, by the way she acted, when he spoke the way she silenced, the way she would warn us when we did or acted a certain way, not necessarily naughty but; of that he does not like. Even down to her way of walking and eating when she ever ate and her facial expression too also; showed discomfort. Her souls seemed sad and disappointed in a certain way that it also; showed me that she was scared and had had enough of life. I felt and picked up the energy she carried in her; it affected me how she felt, and how my siblings felt. She was a very beautiful woman with high class, and very well composed and groomed; she carried so much compassion in her heart, all my friends at school who ever met my mother used to tell me 'your mum is so beautiful and nice, I wish she was my mum', and I used to simply reply; saying "thank you"; with a smile on my visage. Those; friends did not know that my smile was not only of appreciation of their kind words about my mother for her, but it was me also, hiding from their eyes my mother's pain sad life, sad and unhappy marriage and my bothering. She was not happy, but she pretended to be okay, and fine to everyone including her own family; they do not know the depths of what she and Lelo have been going through and what it does to me also; how we have always lived as a family; or what it has been like. With the development of time, findings are that I have also; been a victim of my father and his family. Just like; Mother and Lelo he strategized for his plans and works never to be known and noticed his plan were to catch all of us. One after the other...

His strategy was good for somebody like him and; short legged as it is written in the Bible, and as my mother always says; "'What is hidden in the dark will surely come to light'"; our lives is like a discovery channel. Whatever; is done in the dark does not remain in the dark, GOD brings it to light.

One cannot play judge lest they have walk on the same road or has been elected and risen as so. Still; till today we are going through it, as what I now go through seems to be a continuity and transference of Lelo's relationship with Malto.

Her motherly love, smooth heart and open arms that are always open to everyone. A married woman, who works two jobs at times three or four to sustain her whole household, including her husband, while all he does is, sleep, eat, and sit to watch television, when he speaks he only speaks negativity, oppression and reproaches to others lives. We all have been cursed one time if we were lucky, and if we were not lucky; we have been cursed more then once with his negative words of his evil wishful thinking about all of us for us, which he spoke and still speaks to our lives, claiming that, the Holy Spirit of GOD had spoken to him, and that he is not here to please anyone 'that; we already knew. You will never please anyone', I used to say to myself. And, he curses us with his action that created stumbling blocks to our lives. When someone at home made a plan of progress for himself or herself and he finds out about, he crashes it, and he has crushed mine, Lelo's and my mother's many times. And, then he says that GOD did not want it to happen, or the Holy Spirit told him to do so.

Many times I felt like I was caged, and locked in a prison sell without window and door to escape; and unable to get close to the main door entrance with, no light to see. Left feeling trapped, alike my mother she was very lonely, and she did not have friends, or a social circle, and I was always lonely however; with few friends though few but; still cared not about me, as long as I was not dying. For; that reason they were also undeserving of my friendship, and I was patient and kind to them 'I was left one out, who's presence did, but was not necessary 'a spoiler in some ways"; I did not understand why they did so weird was the word. But; never was I alone. My mum always told me that; GOD always listens to the children, and always encouraged me to pray to GOD, she used to tell me that; Jesus is your saviour and to GOD you can tell and ask him anything. Indeed that; He listens to children. And, she spoke to my siblings and me about love that was an everyday topic of her mouth to us apart from education. It was either scolding us "vôces não se amão porque? (Why don't you love each other?)"; sounding disappointed, hurt, heart broken to find us fighting or arguing about everything and anything that we lucked knowledge and understanding to communicate to each other about the problem. She taught us to be united and to love each other and, to love others.

Whilst her spouse slept at night and woke up in the morning saying, "GOD spoke to me, and told me not to give Lelo anything or money"; wow! I became confused within myself, thoughts automatically started to run through my mind and a thirst to understand the connection between the divinity of GOD's holiness full of love and compassion for the entire world to my dad's prophesy but; I also knew that his prophesies were and still are false; 'would GOD tell a father to do such?' Not to our surprise he had also; stopped supporting Lelo, he truly believed his façades and still does believe that; the revelations he spoke of had truly come from GOD, and they were not another fabrication he created to update himself as a prophetic born again Christian man who GOD uses just; as I always saw it to be. I was astonished, and

I found it to be very ridiculous; the type of bravery my father has, and his fearlessness for GOD to be playing and putting GOD's name in his mouth and defile GOD's character. However; is not surprising because; If a man that is not faithful to his wife, and to his GOD given duties to take care of his children, will he be faithful to GOD?

This had happened few years before we moved to 143 Friars Wood, where life became hell, we were living in a hotel as a family when we first arrived in England, I am the last member of the family to have arrived in England to join the family. But; life had really started to be hell the moment Malto came to join Juliana and my sibling in England, before I also came to join the family. Family life was already hell back home in the motherland, but nobody thought it would ever take its turn to the worst the way it had. My mother thought that things were going to be different with my father, I did not think anything.

It says in the Bible 'Ask and it shall be given to you according to the measure of your faith', if an adult who is full of sins greater then a child and can ask GOD what he wants, and GOD will give him or her what is asked for and wanted, according to his and hers faith. How much more would GOD give to a child? A child victim of that same adult who GOD forgave and who now says that; the Holy Ghost moves him. And; for that adult who is a father and says that GOD the Father has spoken these words to him for his son, and be hatefully towards his child why didn't he intercede for his son, pleading with GOD in prayer for his son to be forgiven of anything wrong he had done, that displeased GOD? From that alone I saw hatred in my dad and that the issue is much deeper then what it seems in the flesh. It is spiritual. He described his encounter with the Holy Spirit about Lelo a pre adolescent kid again with a voice of hatred, anger, pride, and arrogance just like; how he looked like when he assaulted and abused Lelo mentally, physically with his punches and emotionally depriving him from having a father to love and accept him, just as he is... His flesh and blood. GOD is love not hatred, He is unity and not division; GOD speaks the language of multiplication; and this is shown in the holy trinity; Father, Son and Holy Spirit as one GOD, and the son reigns at the right hand side of the father on the throne interceding for you and whom before His glory GOD came down in the full human flesh becoming the son of GOD Jesus Christ through a women in natural birth to walk and live like us, so that HE may understand our burdens, oppression, problems, to die for us and uplifting it all from our lives; all that was weighing down on us. He diligently in obedience to GOD paid the highest price for us, that He came to save us making way for us to go to the father, but was and still is unified with GOD, GOD did not do that because HE wanted to punish HIS only begotten son, HE wanted us, and the glory back to HIM through Jesus Christ, and it took perfection, full holiness divine love. GOD had laid the path for Jesus before He came down, and this is not a punishment; it was a mission to save us. Remember Jesus was also human. Jesus Christ is not sitting or standing at the bottom, at the back feet of the Father in heaven He is beside GOD. And, yet a simple example of love and unity from GOD in heaven the; trinity doesn't get into a self-righteous man who says that he is the GOD elected of the family; one because he is the father, and GOD only speaks to him and no one else because he is the head of the family and the last of it is that; he had read the Bible from A to Z and he knows a lot of things. Indeed he does know a lot of thing, and he also forgets that confession is a vital step of deliverance. But yet he treats his son in the opposite way of how God himself treats his only beloved son. The Bible says that 'HE so love the world that HE gave HIS only son' GOD did not only give his son to be gloried, but to save us all. 'How ironic of this man'; I always thought. He speaks as if he has accepted and received Christ Jesus in his life, heart and soul, and yes he is the first person to also drive his son to sinful, distractive, and a path of pain and suffering where only darkness is found; in search of peace and love. He opened the door for the devil to have him for satan.

A single negative word is enough to open the door and let satan in and destroy a house and one's life, especially when that negative word comes from your own blood and flesh.

"Vai morer, ta brincar, tu es nada carralhio (go die, are you playing, you are nothing (swear word!)"; Malto told Lelo many times.

Making everyone in the house do hard work and subjected Lelo to what I call under parental authority domestic slavery surveillance and hard labour at home. Winter times were the worst Lucianna recalls; the freezing weather crisping up her fingers, her hands left without motion, and her feet and face without feeling, she wished they didn't have to do such; it was every two to three weeks all throughout the year, then years. Most of the times Lelo and I hardly wore coats because; we thought that; it would get in the way of our hard work, but the hard work did not make us warm. We both used the wrongs equipment to clean up a garden, cut the grass, and the branches; thank GOD! There were not flowers in the garden. We cut the grass and the branches with; a kitchen knife and to clean removing remainder and cut of grasses and branches as well as anything that made the garden look dirty or, so we used our bare hands and a broom, and off into the bin bad we had to clean put away the rubbish while we were labouring, and then to the bin outside the house. He also forced and commanded Lelo to fulfil what is meant and known to be a father's duty at home, and society as a provider or protector. Although Malto is the man and father of the house and; he is meant to fulfil these duties. Fixing things, and making sure that he hadn't gone to bed without doing what a father is supposed to be doing, to help mother take care of the house and the children to make the house a safe and healthy environment, go to work. He should have authority however; never without having affection for his wife and children to a certain level.

Malto never did that as a father, because he was and still is a very selfish, arrogant, proud man, and a dictator.

One day, the Lucianna and her family went out on a casual occasion familiy outing in a nice calm Spring day, but when the family had returned to the house the house stunk of pooh; this happened many times. Malto was the only one in the house when they had left for the outing before; Juliana had gone out with the children she had left the house very tidy especially the bathroom and the toilets, and its loos were clean. Lucianna remembers that her and Lelo helped their mother to clean parts of the house, as always; that is part of they daily chores. Sometimes Lucianna and her brother would take each a bathroom and a toilet, they also tided their bedrooms up though most of the times Lelo would avoid to tide his room, and they would both share the living room as Juliana took on the much heavier chores, but for most days Juliana did the whole house by herself as, most good mothers do. 'So, there is no way that one of the toilet was left dirty and smelly with pooh in the loo'.

As; we walked into the house the smell in the house was very bad, that smell was as loud as a Lion roaring wild noise and it smelled as bad as an animal pooh or so, comparable to the smell of a horse's pooh. Yak! The upstairs toilet loo was smudged with pooh; it was all dirty and smelly. My mum saw that and was so disgusted in fact every one of us saw it, and my father started saying that he also; found the toilet in that disgraceful state, and then he started exclaiming that it was Benjamin; my youngest brother who was then two years and a half who did that. I quietly said within myself 'liar', Benjamin was still wearing his nappies, not to a full time, but he always called for assistance when he wanted to use the toilet like; a big boy, and when he sneaked into the bathroom it was just because; he wanted to wash his hands, and he didn't think anyone's help was needed the loo was only useful to Benjamin for a hand wash...

"Benjamin was a one of a kind child, throwing clothes outside the window, or putting it in the bin... he would, the technical apparels around the house and putting them back together, by fixing it himself; rejecting help especially to getting told";

I used to laugh at the things he used to do, there was just no way one could get mad at him; it was impossible. And, he used to say "I'm too little I can't reach the sink"; in his wobbly voice and tone. We used to tell him to call us and, not to wash your hand in the loo. And his hands my mother used to rewash and disinfect them straight after we found out he had been to the toilet, or he had been to the toilet although; most of the time he was the one to come to us and tell us about his hand washes missions to the toilet. I always found it funny.

If, anyone didn't do Malto's will, then this person was condemned to unavoidable harsh beatings, punishments, or insults to being bullied. I never really received any beatings from father, but whatever portion I received, Junior got it one hundred times worst above my portion; not even to talk and think of the beatings "Vroohohh, fogo". He would beat him as tough one is giving beatings to kill an adversary, and not of a father correcting his son since; there was not wrongs done by Lelo to had deserved those beatings. Or; a father wanting the best for his son as; the excuse many African parents present before, after and while the beating, especially the ones that were born and brought up in African villages.

'I am beating you because I want the best for you!!!' and there it goes with the metal end of the belt, the punches, the kicks on the butt, some parents actually kick in the butt, and claim to love their children, like that. 'I love you, that is why I'm beating you'; how many people have heard this phrase before?

Lelo has been underfoot crashed in the face by my father before and kicked on the head while he was down. I remember Lelo was asleep the night this happened, and Malto felt that he should teach Lelo a lesson since he was fifteen years old and still living at home. Malto kicked Lelo on the head when Lelo was in bed sleeping, after he arrived home late at two in morning after Valentine's Day.

Malto saw that to be the perfect, and justifying excuse to beat and mal treat Lelo the way he did and all of us at the same time; but he failed to see that people who knew of our family problem understood the type of father and man he is and he cannot hide forever. A dictator, children and wife slave owner, adulterer, selfish, violent, aggressive, arrogant, self-centred father that he has always been. And I was right; I saw all this, for the most part I kept quiet... but; nothing of gracious he did as a falsity in front of those who knew the problems faces, hid his true persona that; many failed and still are failing to see.

Sometimes, Lucinna wishes for everyone to find out the hypocrite, and false person that her father is, she thinks of that moment that everyone who looks at her dad and thinks that he is the definition of honest and righteous man suddenly; discover that he is far from what they highly think of Malto. Although; she also wishes that he is better then what he truly is; so that she would not feel this way.

He spends hours on the phone helping by giving advices, and educating other peoples children that; of his family. His nephews and nieces in Africa and all over around the world wherever they might be, with such a passion and love of one who is a much better father to his own children, when in fact he doesn't even notice his own children best interest. Lucianna recalls a phone conversation when he was advising his brother in law not to give money to his children if they ask, because they don't need it, and when he got on the phone to his nephews he spoke a different language.

To the extend of degrading his son over a love he thinks to be much more valuable to him and life then his love for his son, and a good healthy father and son relationship he could have had with his son if he was a fit and loving father rather then a fit candidate for dictatorship.

"You will see, you think I'm amusing with you? I will send you back to Africa, I will chuck you there and leave you there for you to starve and you will be a street kid, and I will not send you not a dime for you to live by and on. You will see"

"I will teach you how to live. You will see how you will suffer. You think I care about you? Wait, I'll show you. I'll send you back! You will go to Cabinda, and my nephew will come to live here, he is much better then you! Do you think he is dumb like you? He is clever! Do you understand?"

Time after times, he had exalted himself with anger and, hatred to say this things to Lelo with a boiling blood, thirsty and ready as he always threatened to spank Lelo saying "I'll spank you! What are you looking at?" or "I'll spank you, what are you doing here?", Lelo could have only past through by the living room from the kitchen to go upstairs to his room, stood up still to watch the program passing on the television, or having a laughter with us; me my mum, and younger siblings. That was enough wrong in Malto's eyes and mind for him to go at Lelo with blows and insults, get his belt out and throw a chair at him. They were very intensive and disturbing scene; there was so much aggression, and hatred. Poor Lelo never said a word or did anything to defend himself, he couldn't because he could have become a murdered case. He was scared, always scared, and grew tired of hiding it, but never spoke about it. My heart; always broken for him every day, and I didn't know how to consolidate him. My brother.

I used to think that boys didn't like to play with girls because, girl are girls, soft and emotional. So, I learned to play football by watching my brother and the neighbourhood boys, who where actually older then me, and some were also older then Lelo;

but just so I could play with my brother and cheer him up, whenever he let me hang out with him. That used to happen a lot in Luanda. He was very alone, he felt alone and unhappy; everywhere and anywhere we have been in the world. I remember when we were younger, and we used to make plan to run away from home if my dad didn't change sooner, especially him. The first time we spoke of doing a runner was on a evening, my dad was at work at his military squad of FAA, my mother was in the living room with my aunty, and her boyfriend who is now her husband, they were watching television and there was no maid or nanny in the house by that time as their work shift hours had already finished for the day. My aunty and my uncle better then anyone they know how my dad is and was back then, though many years have passed and we have not seen and coexisted together like in the years of my childhood, she still knows him very well. She remembers and worries about us, especially about Lelo.

In the kitchen we were, whispering whenever we spoke, Lelo had a much more feminine voice then me, I was loud at the age of six, and my voice was loud and smooth like the voice of a big baby. We both started the conversation on our 'run away subject', and we used to call it 'operation plan'; my mother knew nothing about our plan, and I used to think that our plan was perfect, however it saddened me at times because; I didn't want to grow up in the streets and become a street kid and homeless I used to panic at the thought of becoming poor motherless and fatherless; and I used to think

'How and where will I have my daily bath, what about my clothes? They will be dirty, and I don't want to be dirty; will I have to carry a suitcase around, and what about food and going to school?'

My answer for food was that; we can take lots of fruits with us from home when we run away, so we can eat fruits everyday and still be healthy. "We will take a lot of fruits!"; I used to say, and I used to try to visualise how my brother would look like too; on the long term after we ran away from home, and what we would be like if we didn't find any solutions to the thoughts that were in my mind. Sometimes, my mind would travel in my head wondering around for solutions and it often took me back to why I didn't want my brother to runaway and become a street kid, and poor; like me if I had left with him. But; it also reminded me that we were not happy at home, and I thought about the suffering part Lelo was undergoing at home, not being happy and then; to escape for happiness and, still not find any happiness. I couldn't find Lelo happy as a street child in my imagination, instead I saw him poor like me in the street, and I asked myself 'how, and why are two kids from a family of wealthy status and high influence be doing in the street?'; this is what I also, thought people would say in their minds after seeing us living, sleeping, seated in the street and begging for change... And I did not see myself ready for that.

'What is Lelo thinking?'; I used to try to get into his mind and find out but; of course it was impossible. I felt like he really wanted to get away from suffering and maltreats that was going on at home, but he also understood that it would be tough for us to live alone. Every time I looked at my brother I saw a great brother and a great man of the future, inside all the questionable thought that I had about us running away. As; scary as the thoughts were for me; I also, felt that my big brother would not have left me starve, or live without an education although; I also knew that; he was not going to be able to pay the tuition fees for me, or his own as, we were still kids, but I envisioned him trying, and making a better future for both of us. If we did runaway; our parents would have found us easily; my dad was going to shake the whole country and turn it up side down to find us.

"meus filhos! Aonde astão os meus filho!? Qhem levou os meus filhos?!" this is what dad would say.

Lucky, the person who ever wanted to touch us but never did, because if anyone ever touched us? Hmmmmmm they would have suffered, and shit on themselves everyday of the rest of their lives. My father was a very respectable authority because; of his position in society, his job and of course everything that happened in our home stayed in between the walls of the house. Till this day in the; whole of the country amongst the authorities and certain parts of the country and some other countries in the world; he is still known and respected. Nobody; messed with him, the family or anybody known to have been associated to our family, because of his military power, authority, influences and the family money. The money talked; but it came through my mum's hard work and success not Malto's.

Malto's way of thinking is 'only I can touch my family and no one else'; and it doesn't matter if you do to us what he does to us. Because; if you are an outsider or an extended family member trying to or are treating us the way he does, less or worst, then you are over; unless he has allowed you to.

Lucianna thinks that her dad is a predator that acts in the family, not to the outsiders out of cowardly sentiments. A predator signifies: subjects that according to them as individuals must climb on others, back to get ahead in life; is a carnivore animal characteristic also reflected on humans.

I hardly called Lelo Big brother 'mano', but when we had our conversations to strategise our operation plan to runaway; I automatically called him 'mano' it felt good to call him that. Felt weird.

Before we held our private meeting for our operation plan; he used to tell me as, a reminder we had a meeting... And, during our operation plan he used to say "at midnight hours when everyone is sleeping"; and I used to re alliterated after him "at midnight hours when everyone is sleeping"; and he continued "we'll jump out your bedroom window, but don't make any noise"; and I copied him again "we'll jump out my bedroom window, and I won't make noise"; continuing saying if we make noise dad will catch us, and he will beat us hard, but I knew that I was probably not going to get beatings from my father, but Lelo was going to get beaten extremely hard. But that time I was not scared just worried, I didn't find it fair for him to take the blame alone when we planned the operation together. Especially that I was excited to run away; that would have been my first adventure, and lone late night outing; I thought.

It was fun; I used to get excited when the time to talk about the operation came about. It used to make me feel intelligent, and I used to think that I was a Russian spy in some ways. I became vigilant and watchful by, watching what people were doing at day time night at home or at school and then I reported to Lelo in case if we found more space to runaway during day light rather; then for us to run away at midnight. After; a while Lelo and I no longer took the plan seriously I guess we both knew we did not have the courage to do that, and put our parents under stress, especially my mom. But; then he branded me as a 'reporter', but that wasn't for too long till my little sister came around our house to start living with us.

Essa is her name; the first time I saw her, she was six months old, and I asked my mother who she was "Mãmã quem é essa bébé? (Mother who is this baby girl?)"; my mother replied me saying that she was my sister, I asked my mother further questions

...

"Ela stava aonde? (Where were she?)"; I asked my mother

"Hospital", she replied, and I asked her "Como é que eu não te ví gravida, mas eu não te ví ir no hospital (How come I did not

see you pregnant, plus I did not see you going to the hospital)";
and then she told me she had her when she went to Congo on a
business trip. Mmm, mmmm mmm I was thinking; that did not
add up to me at all. Instantly; at meeting Essa I knew that she
was not my full blood biological sister, I could tell; I found her to
be a weird baby, different but not in a positive way; I had never
seen a baby as skinny as she was and rude at the same time
like; an adult caged in a baby's body. She looked; weak and sick,
and for some reason I did not feel that sisterly love connection
out of my soul toward her as my sister. Like; how I loved Lelo
but; I also felt the same regards coming from her, although she
was a baby but; the connection is very important to ones type
of relationship. I did not feel like she was my full sister at time
not even my half sister; I felt gutted because; before she came
around, I really wanted a sister. Though; I called her my sister
and not stepsister. I always told people that 'she is my sister';
when it was asked, or if I presented to people outside our home.

She had wide big eyes, long thin face; and every time I looked
at her to me; she looked like an Ethiopian or Rwandan girl. She
refused to eat at all time, she seemed to be in agony and panic,
Essa seemed to have a savage spirit as she would have a go at
people who were; from home especially me, and she used to
scratch me, try to bite me and throw objects at me example;
her toys. I remember once she punched me and my front teeth
fell out, Lelo laughed at me, my uncle did too, my mother did
not care much about that. She was seated on the floor playing,
and I went over to play with her too, as soon as she saw me
seated to play with her she screwed at me, and I found it weird
that a baby knew and would do adults expressions; the way she
did it. But I still wanted to play with her. I sooner found out
that I had made the wrong move.

I often told my mother she was weird, and the things she used
to do were strange, especially that; she did them. I remember
I also used to tell my mother that; I think she lied about that

baby that came to my house. Essa was not her daughter; in her defence she always attempted to make sure that is clear that she is her daughter, and my full blood sister.

I did not understand know why, but I could never take what she said serious, plus my Russian spy instinct was already awaken and never went to sleep again as far as this subject was not clarified.

Lucianna tried to adding things up. Her mother had told her that her supposed full blood baby sister was a premature baby, and that she had given birth to Essa when she was six months pregnant in Congo. That part to Lucianna was one of the major parts of the story her mother told her that brought disbelieve toward her mother; in relation to her sister's case. Things did not seem to be as clear as they were told to Lucianna, and she found no point in asking her father about that new baby girl in the family, because he was not going to say anything about the truth.

Over the years as Lucianna grew up she has discovered the characteristics of her father, and learned not to rely on his version of the truth when she asked him about things. So I asked not questions! When Malto hesitated to tell the truth about any question she had and had asked him; he simply didn't give an answer, but instead swerved her off to her mother to ask the question for an answer or explanation "ask your mother"; till today he does that, she thinks in concordance to her siblings thoughts of that too. "He puts us in the middle of the problems he has and creates for himself with my mother to hide his mess and ugly characters, but he cannot hide because; we know who he is"; says Lucianna, to a different degree, she now sees his personality and character with wider opened eyes.

He does things, and lies about his actions, role-play and participation in it, by hiding behind somebody in silence or; trying to undress himself of the blame creating a situation that whoever he hides behind then get the blame. Usually the person he often hides behind happens to be my mother; poor innocent women, but she also; knows not to get involved in his problems; and issues, but he always involves her. As soon as; things get heated on his side then he hides behind his wife, and bringing her name up in his arguments as his alibi, and other people, whoever he thinks would be the great spokes person for him, and if he finds it necessary depending on his defence strategy.

Lucianna therefore stopped asking her mother question about it; the sudden surfacing of her sister, and if a question based on her sister topic slipped out of her mouth the question was "is she really your daughter?"; but she also, precipitately answered the question to herself for her mother "no she is not your daughter, you know it and so do I"; not allowing anymore space for pretends by her mother.

The answer to Lucinna's questions were confirmed to her many years after the first sixth years of Essa's when first came to her house as a six months old baby. Essa and Lucianna never got along, Lucianna always caught her with her lies and, she also portrayed attention seeking behaviour and attitude, but Lucianna seemed to be the only one to have had noticed Essa like that. But; the strange thing is that, no one in her home saw, decided to overlook at things regarding Essa's character, behaviour, personality and attitude especially Julianna. Lucianna thinks her mother chose to blind herself from the true characteristics of Essa and defended her at all costs, more then she has ever defended Lucianna, and she think that she did that out of fear of her father and her crave to stay in the good book of her husband Malto; meanwhile she has never been his favour as his wife. She denied herself and her own birth children for her marriage to her husband, and her stepdaughter was always first before her birth biological daughter. Essa is a stranger that came into her house and family as a fruit of dishonesty and infidelity from of her parent, as so she imagined, before she found out about which; one of her parents is the unfaithful one although; she already knew it all, but in this case the battle was for the truth not to be hidden.

Lucianna always brags about her natural instincts to her-self "my instincts are never wrong"; she tells herself. As Essa started to grow up till this stage of her life; her face, personality, and character also became clearer as to who she really resembles alike. What she thought, and saw about Essa many years ago; she now also sees that she was right about her sister as ever so regarded her as, at acceptance to her.

To Lucianna that; was enough evidence to prove to her without a word of confirmation that; they were not full blood sisters; although she already knew that they were not she... Still kept quiet. And, proud of her mother for everything she had gone through and keeping GOD's status in her heart and life, making her to see not the point and reason to reject the truth although; Lucianna also; wishes that the truth was not hidden for so long either. The truth she always knew hurt Lucianna, she saw many mistakes of her mother pointing to her rather then her mother or her father and of the times her stepsister too, by the choices her mother made and her silence and the causer of her mother's pain and unhappiness. Lucianna did not find it to be fair. The negligence she felt from her mother towards her; for many years of her life, but whenever she dares try to talk about it to her mother, and to bring to her attention what and how she felt or was made to feel; Julianna's responses are as if; those things Lucianna felt and lived are all imaginative. Showing; the luck of interest in the conversation, she swerved away the topic as though, she knew of how she treated Lucianna but; feeling ashamed to admit and look back at the choices she made. She sees the hurt of many years in her daughter; but she cannot go back in time.

Many at times Lucianna felt like her mother served her; as the maid and the stepdaughter to her will and at her siblings' service, and to Essa who is the stepdaughter.

"Although there are two sides of this; I know that one side was to train me as a girl, but the other side is how my mother did it... my brother saw it and for his amusement he labelled me 'slave'; for fun, but I didn't like it"

Different from her father as; he gave and still gives zero tolerance. In many ways Lucianna believes that her mother did that to her with good intentions for her:

"But it didn't always feel good to be ignored and treated as though what I had to say didn't matter, and to be made fun of"; says Lucianna. She remembers her mother siding up with her brother when he made fun of her. Sometimes; Lucianna thinks that Juliana used it as punishment on her to pour her grieve out, why did it had to be her daughter? Because she is a female like her and what she went through her daughter might go through it one day. But she did it with harshness 'is how she did it'; that made Lucianna think that; it was punishment and resentment towards her, and Lucianna was also; very loved by her father, and her father is the person who hurt Julianna... but he didn't get punished, and she had no one else but me, after her sister returned back to her husband every evening, when we left Luanda, when we lost Lelo because of Malto, I was there, it was me but GOD first. But Julianna also did not grow up with her mother.

Nevertheless, Lucianna always had dreams, good dreams, dreams of always having a good, happy, respectable, rich and wealthy life; many times those dreams diverted her mind from a four corners closed in walls without a door to escape she lived in. Her mother never did fully pay attention to her; leaving her to feel resentment from her mother; there was no friendship and proximity of mother and daughter relationship. But nobody knew it, and they still don't know this side of their relationship was Lucianna's pain and battle for victory. My brother; Lelo used to tell me with sarcasms in his tone of voice and with what he used to say, whilst also making fun of me saying "you Love to dream isn't it Lucianna, so when are you going to be a Politian?"

"Why don't you just become one?"; but I think he appreciated the fact that I was passionate about life and a positive person at that young age. Many young girls of that age I was in; had fallen to destruction. Lelo once told Lucianna "don't be desperate for friends."

The Different Influences I

Instead of her being desperate for friends she strived for GOD and, desperate she was for GOD.

He told me this after making fun of me; which is something that he always did. He told me that I had no friends, and afterwards he dropped an eye and mind opening discernment phrase by saying "don't be desperate for friends"; and I remember his face when he said this to me; it was full of amusement as he continually took the meek out of me. It was truthful what he had told me; I never really had a friend to call friend and that I could claim to be my best friend though; most of the time others claimed me to be their best friend without my approval, and I just went along with it. Until the day it came across him. I was not the only person Lelo used to make fun of; sometimes Lelo would also take the meek out of my friends, and other girls at school. I used to feel very sorry for some of those girls who got laughed at by my brother. He called them ugly with a typical boy attitude, not that he thought that he was good looking himself; just a boy doing a boy type of behaviour is. Lelo then became a little bit vein in our days of high school; I used to catch him talking to himself in front of the mirror at home in the upstairs bathroom. Caressing is chin and, liking his lips as if he was so handsome, and there was a girl he stood and looked at himself in the mirror for hours. I used to laugh at him when he was taking his self-admiration spa sessions at home in front of a mirror.

There was a group of Nigerian and Ghanaian girls we went to school with and were in my brother year group they were called ugly, and told to be trying so hard to look sexy by Lelo, he really bothered them but; the irony was that they liked him so much even after he bothered them. Me, on the other hand as his other victim; I used to get called fat girl and baby elephant by him, and I remember I used to think that by this age that I am now; the names calling would have stopped. I was wrong!

I never found it funny I used to want to beat him up and I used to tell him "you're lucky you're my big brother if you weren't I would have beaten you up long time ago... I pity you that; is why I have not done it yet"; and he used to laugh whenever I said that and I still did not find it funny. But he did. You can not even be perfect not to be bothered by Lelo, he has a problem with girl who wear make up, put extension on their hairs, and girls who wear clothes that are figure hugging; girls who do not wear make up and who did not wear tight clothes are grandmas to him. Sometimes I don't blame Lelo for troubling the girls or women that choose to reveal their body with too short or too tight clothes and the girls who did not choose to do so, not that I assume they all had a choice. He is just a man saying in description what he sees.

The way a women, young women, pre adolescent or a girl dresses, carries herself in public, or in private place were there are other people in attendance; the way they display themselves shows others, especially man which are the main audience of those mini supper tight skirt, how much she self values and self-respects herself. I don't think is always, or only due to the manner she is dressed but; I think that her attitude counts; is what speaks louder then her dress code. As judgemental as it is; and as Lelo sounded at times, Lucianna believed that; the things Lelo used to say would not have been said if they hadn't been so much of a displayed of flesh from one particular female or group of girls.

Fashion is an art topic and self-respect and value are another topic, however they can both coexist within one body of soul and be manifested together as one. Have you ever heard of the expression 'what you wear is what you are'? Lucianna has always been for freedom of expression just as, fashion is also a way to express freedom, believes and choices of life through creativity in clothing.

I remember when I was fourteen years old, and almost all the other girls I saw of my age were following the same fashion styling trend; that promoted sex appeal it was not only fourteen years old girls; it was girls between the age of twelve to sixteen and seventeen years of age girls. They were following the crowed; you know! The street dress code and fashion style which; was the trend at the time that; it had also take its stage in schools premises. I described the trend to be school sex appeal, although I don't think that some girls were dressing that way to attract the boys at school but it seemed like it. For example; the friend I had in school were always flattered whenever; the older and gangster boys at school approached them, when they wore mini skirt school uniform. They wore tight or flirty, and very short skirts and walked in provocative manner while, they passed through the school corridor, in the playground they flirtatious and attention seekers. The boys used to love to see that. I in the other hand grew up differently with my siblings; Uche and Benjamin are now teenagers, but they don't give attention to girls who dress that way; they keep themselves grounded. The sexy standards of teenage girls, and young women has now become something that; male adults focus on, rather then young teenage boys nowadays from my observations on my brothers, and the young boys I see around. Skin-tight clothes all year along and every day. Some girls; wore hooded sleeveless short coats, and trainers, converses, Gucci shoulder bag everywhere for those who could afford it; that is if they were real Gucci. Girls had piercings, on their face: side of upper lips, nose piercing, tongue piercing, and multiple ears piercing. For the sexy bad girl look.

The hair trend was also very important; because it completed the look. Everyone used gel and sleeked their hair on a side part, and up in a ponytail. There were girls, incorporated germs on their hairs sticking it with hair gel on their baby hairs; as part of their hairstyle. My friend used to go as far as writing her name at her side part fringe she used to gel her hair, with fancy lettering, and it looked sick! Bad...

The words sick and bad, when I was growing up were used to express good, nice, phenomenon and amazing. It was a way to compliment something or somebody for the beauty and creativity or anything admirable. My friend; who was actually the only person ever doing that hairstyle with her name written on her gelled side fringe; with gems as part of the hairstyle. She took to the next level.

Apart from the dominant trend hairstyle, there were three dominant trends in the London borough of Croydon; where I grew up; tong boys was one of the style and fashion trend that many girls took on, they completely dressed like boys from head to toes in boys clothes, mainly tracksuits, hoodies and trainers, they also behaved like delinquent street boys, going around stealing, inappropriate behaviour in public, criminal damage, beating people in the street, fighting both girls and boys and making agreements to scuff students from other schools. I've never witnessed any afterschool fight between two different schools but I always heard stories about the beef between high schools. To me; tong boys' girls, were girls who lucked confidence to look as 'sexy and feminine', or lucked confidence in whom they are; fashion and socially wise they lost themselves by identifying themselves as boys, and being marginalised.

Tong boy girls also wore the boys casual wear assemble of denim and trainer's half way laced up with tie knot, buggy t-shirt and jumper that hid the female silhouette. I had a best friend whom I had met at my old church I met her and her sister, they were always together, if one went home without the other they would be in trouble. She had a tong boy sister; which was normal at the time as that was the trend for many girls, but there were times that I used to think that she was a lesbian. Of course I never made any comments on that to anyone. It was not my business. I dated the same boy she wanted to date, or maybe she dated him before he dated me and from the day she heard about me and the boy she still liked; she started to hate me. She did not tell me that she hated me, but I knew, by the way she had began to treat me with a childish resentment as if I was her rival. If she saw me down needing help she would look and pass by as if she knew not me; but I did not care about how she treated me I was not close to her, and never wanted to be so.

It is something about Lucianna and the way she always curried her self, regardless of the people around her and their influences attempted to be inflicted on her to impact the course of her life, well being, mental health, character, personality and innocence; but she was way wiser then most young girls of her age. She has always been a very; strong-minded individual to the extent that others malice's against her was brought down to nothing and would become as if nothing is going on like; the ground she stepped on before her and them. What her friends did is not what she did, and what everybody did is not what she followed and wanted for herself; as she always felt that "those things were a waist of time for me"; says Lucianna. Many young girls life is destroyed due to their surrender to destructions, many of these girls and a few she once knew by encounter in church, and being in the youth group; where she met other youths and many of the time these youths had their own destructive ways.

"Be careful with whom you walk with Lucianna, Lelo. Many people who go to church don't go for GOD, they are there with a mission, and to complete their mission"

Juliana always told Lucianna and her big brother Lelo many people go to church to bring destruction, just like; there are many of their kind out there in the world, "be vigilant and keep yourself to yourself with God and don't follow your friends".

My mother was right I saw many things, and went through many adversities, not only of the flesh but; most of my adversities brought to me and against me by; my adversaries were of the spirit. My former best friend was an adversary; but not of the flesh because; I did not consider her to be one although she often stood as an opposition to me; however she was an adversary of the spirit. She had; imprudent and ungodly ways; which I did not want to partake with her nor; did I want to be impacted by her ways. I knew who I was, I knew already at a young age although I was not clear and as sure; but I knew who I am, I knew and believed in GOD's plan for my life, and I still believe and know that there is much more for me from GOD almighty; the ELOIME, the GOD of Israel. I had a vision for my life and I did not let anyone rob me from it I held on to it and; I am still holding on amidst all the adversaries I face daily. Whenever I corrected my ex best friend Tamy about her wrong ways and destructions; she used to act like she did not care because; it was her life, and as far as she was concerned I had no right to speak to her, about her conduct, or advise her even as; her 'best friend'. I remember she told me to shut up once; and on other occasions I could almost hear her heart out yelling at me to shut up; I could tell and feel what; she was longing to tell me or do 'make me shut up'. The looks in her face and the way she turned her face to blank me, just like she did with other people she had issues with; and then turned to me to tell me what she thought of the person she happened to fight with. I knew her. Tamy hang out with people who were associated with people who ran the streets, who's main focus was the streets; in certain towns of Croydon although; there was a part of me that wanted to know these people, especially the girls. I also; wanted to have more friends and be popular at times that; was my definition of social acceptance, and to be able to relate in a better ways with Tamy; as I wanted to know what the streets

45

were like. But I also had displeasure of coming to know about the deep and dark hidden side about it. The person in whom I so called best friend; used to pretend not to know me in public when she had her top girls, bad girls friends in her company; but when we were at church and she had no money and she was hungry on the Sundays afternoon after church service I was her best friend ever, then she acknowledged me, and wanted to be close to me. The girls she knew and trusted so much, and hang out with used to look at me as if I was not much but a nobody; an idiot and just as stupid as anybody who did not live their lifestyle... I now; look back at those times, and I smile 'ironic; they must had thought that they were looking in the mirror; seeing themselves and, talking back at themselves'; as I was the educated one with a picture of where I want to go in life, and I was educated, and they were otherwise. This; happened every time I was with Tamy or when Tamy was with me, and it was weird because; whenever we were seen together or where at same location, our crossroad friendly meetings happened by coincidence only. Usually; Tamy and I met at the bus station or in the middle of Croydon high street after all; I did not dress like them, speak like them, and walk like them or think like them! I had my own identity and status, I always looked presentable, spoke well although I had an accent, but I always have been educated and I greeted people when I saw them; especially the people I knew. I was the total opposite of those girls and Tamy, but I didn't mind that at all; being different. I knew better then to be desperate for friends.

Some; of these girls really wanted to harm me even though they knew not me, they looked at me with hatred, in attempt to scare me and awake a atrocious behaviour and character out of me because, that is the only way that they would had felt like; they had open doors to do something to me, me showing that I was intimidated by them or, giving satisfaction of how I felt by their words to actions was only going to make them feel strong. Therefore; that did nothing to me as 'I had not done anything to them before they tried me, and I did not give them the satisfaction of acknowledgement after they had tried me'; nor did I know them. The way they spoke to me and the things they have told me; when they had spoken to me showed me what they were and opened my eyes about their sorts of people.

Once, I took the tram from George Street tram stop to West Croydon bus station as I entered the tram, and I was going to seat down a young girl who was older then me by about three to four years, with the name of Mannuela; she was also Tamy's friend she was also; getting on the tram from the same stop as me. She saw me and, she had recognised me and; sat down with me; opposite me, when I saw her, I had also recognised her while we were both seating down on the blue repeated un-functional yellow and orange triangle shaped patterned tram seat; we both complimented each other with a 'Hi!'. Strangely; we had a conversation, although there was not much said by me, but of her telling me of a particular day when she had gone out with the aim to vandalise a clothing shop with her friends by the market near Church Street tram stop. Someone was caught, and the rest of her friends and; herself ran away, leaving the other criminal behind.

She then looked at me in a rude way; rolled her eyes, then looked at me up and down, and told me "nobody will ever see me role with someone like you"; and I said me? She replied saying "yeah you, I will never role with people like you, looking like a nick, me no! Never" "I could robe you right now, I could just punch you up and blow you up";

I was baffled, and thought to myself 'really?'; I did not say anything as she continued to talk seated opposite me while; we were still in the same tram, face to face. I never told anyone about that day, but the words she told me stayed in my mind for some reason.

Lucianna is shock and thoughtful...

It was around the time Lelo my brother; had already formed many friendship with many people; via school, boys we met at our old church, and his friends met through other friends of his. He had one or two good friends which who moved to New Castle and Glasgow, they were best of friends, but did not grow up together; he often dismissed the advices he got from his friends based on choosing good friends, and being careful with his friends; as he was surrounded by bad company after his two best friends left London with their family. Although; he also met again one or two good kids that he called friends, though high school; I didn't like my brother to befriend them; to be walking with bad companies; there were a few particular ones of his friends I did not like and I wanted them away from my brother.

Mannuela was one of the people from the wrong crowed that my brother was attracted to; no! He did not like her or wanted to be her boyfriend or; anything of such, whilst she branded me 'a no body'; she was nobody comparing to the girls friends my brother had in his company. It was the crowed that attracted him. Although; she knew who my brother was by his name 'Lelo'; but they were not friends, or better, Lelo was not her friend that I know.

I described her to be a sad low life in my mind, and a wanna be wishing to climb on my back for higher gang status, financial and materialistic good! By robbing me, but she was scared; somebody greater then her was behind me GOD, and on human level my brother was an excuse for her not to touch me. I asked myself 'did she not dare to touch me or make me her victim on that day, because she knows that I am Lelo's younger sister or, what?'; nevertheless; my life moved on from that encounter with Mannuela.

Many, of the times that I had called Tamy best friend I did not understand and know why I took her as a friend especially; a best friend. I knew nothing about her things. I knew the friend I had, Tamy was not a bad person, but she was also not the best friend friend; she was not worth my friendship after having studied her personality, character, conduct and ways that I did not agree with. For four years of our friendship as best friends; Tamy treated me bad I felt very wronged and let down every time she was supposed to be a friend to me. As, a friend I was there for her when she had problems with her sisters especially with Temirah, and when her mother and stepfather fell out and fought when; there was no food in her house because somehow her parents were unable to provide for her family and she had passed days according to her without food in her stomach. My house was a free restaurant for her and my mother's cooking; a free meal but; when we were out after the youth group meetings, as church was the only place we ever met up. When we were both hungry, she used to sneak into KFC leaving me behind knowing that I was also hungry and had not enough money to buy a proper meal to eat to share with my friend, at times I did no had any money either. "I'm hungry! I don't have money to buy food... Temirah what did mum cook today?"; and mourned saying "mmmm, I'm hungry"; If I was a rude friend, I could have sworn that she was pregnant every day, by the way she used to eat all the time, Tamy ate a lot, but she was not even fat; not skinny either, definitely not skinny.

One day after a Sunday youth meeting, most of us were from the youth group were hungry, but also many went straight home. We used to hang out just outside in front of the church, we could have each gone our separate ways and had eaten in our houses; but it was much more comforting to hang out especially as Lelo also; felt better outside then at home and so did I. Being; that we were fed up of the same things me, Lelo and mother faced every day. We had found a certain type of peace outside of home, and I liked to just see the world moving; people walking, cars being driven on road, buses stopping at bus stops and picking up passengers etc. it was the type of liberty I did not have when I was in Paris, France altogether with the abuse, discomfort, no liberty and the unhappiness at home; I felt better outside, and as long as, Lelo had the fresh air to breathe and a break from the madness at home, the more at peace my mind was; as we were always together.

Alone In Paris

In the plane we sat separately; I sat alone in the middle aisle column stuck between two men, a black tall man and a white blond haired tall man too. I was excited that I was going to fly for the first time before hand, and I was so courageous and fearless; seated alone amongst adults did not fear me although; I was shy very shy. I remember my mother was seated at front left hand side window seat with Benjamin two rows behind her was Lelo and Uche accompanied by a man my mother paid to help her with watching us; and Essa sat in the row in front of her. I was the only child who was seated a little far from everyone in the plane.

The white man kept on looking at me, and each time he looked at me he smiled and I would straight away look away, down on the light blue skirt of the dress I wore on that day, and on my right wrist I wore a thin charming gold bracelet. I never smiled back, it worried me; he was a stranger and my mother always used to tell me not to speak to strangers. I remember whishing 'I whish I was close Lelo'; I was not happy far from my family in the aeroplane. The hostess walked by my aisle back and forth many times; from the back to the front, and all of a sudden the television got turned on! I was getting happy, but I whished that I was holding the remote control so that; I could search the channels and find my interest, I wanted to watch cartoons.

It was midnight sharp; I looked up, and I saw a white slander, golden blond hair women completely naked then; I looked away straight away to my left hand side and, I saw the white, tall, blond hair man softly but briefly from the corner of his eye. I directed my eyes to the front I wanted to go to my mother, but I could no longer see her again; and I thought maybe she went to the toilet or, fell asleep and her head must have leaned over to her shoulder and also adjusted the seat and her body to comfort.

I looked back at the television; I did not want to watch it, but I saw more this time; the woman was kneeled down with a slightly bent back on a bed while beneath her a white man was laying down; he had his hands pressing down on her head, while it was moving up and down. I stared at the television for that short while and, diverted my head again 'Mum will tell me off for seeing this'; I told myself and I looked for sleep but, it never came; instead I got anxiety over being on the aeroplane and arriving in France to live in Paris; for the while we were going to live there. I was so excited about being up high in the clouds, and all I wanted to do is see and touch them, and I cared not even about the food served in the aeroplane; for the first time I felt no interest in food or milk, what I saw did not look appetising; neither was I hungry on that flight journey. I cannot recall having any meal including break fast, or eating anything at my uncle's house before he and his daughter my cousin took us to the airport.

Uncle Marcelo; was one of our two or, favourite uncles, and before we left the country we were living in his three bedrooms flat with his wife, daughter and his brother in law. Before; moving to his house mother had sold everything we had as, agreed between her and my dad; the house, house furniture, cars, lands etc. except from our businesses, which were very much his according to how much of the income mother saw, which was non. Mother; in the other hand left her business to her sister to take care of it, while she was getting away which; her husband has taken over now and he has also extradited my mother from returning to her own created business just because; they have managed to make a lot of money while mother has been away for protection. Mother; also gave some things away to her sister as; they were things of so much value that could not be traded, so instead she gave it to her sister and other relatives who she thought would take good care of them as per their values too. When we left our house nobody saw us leaving; my uncle Marcelo came to our house and, first took our stuff in his car to his house and on his third trip he took my mother, me, Lelo and Benjamin. Uche and Essa where already out of the country with Malto; they were staying at my grandfather's house my mother's father in the now Congo.

In that house; my mother finically sustained it with the money my father left for mother to pay for our visas to France, passports, and living expenses, and to treat us with what we were accustomed to. She; paid for the food, we all ate, and the bills; as they were financially behind their bills especially the rent for their house.

Our last moments in my country were; spent in his house with his family; we were well received by him and his wife. He spoke English but not so well, it was always fun to hear him throwing out the few English words he knew with; Myk his neighbour who was always drunk, and he always embarrassed his daughters because of his drunkenness and jobless lifestyle.

It was as if; I was invisible at the airport; my mother knew not of what to make of me on that day, place and time although; I suspected that she was maybe marvelled at my courage, by the look in her face. Uncle Marcelo was a head pilot back then, and went in to make sure that all went smooth along with a few family friends which; I only knew by names, who made sure to be there for cover, there were strong connections there, but most importantly mother made sure to commit and command our journey in GOD's hand, ans 'Amen' we said at the end of the prayer. That; is the best cover one can attain; is all found in GOD's divine protection. Mother prayed with me, Lelo and Benjamin in the room we were sleeping in; in uncle Marcelo's house before we departed to the airport, I remember she always slept on the floor as; it was her plead to GOD. And; the day before mother's younger sister came to visit us for the final goodbye! '... I really miss her'; even though she made sure to see us all throughout the week going back and forth before we left Angola.

I remember; we used to tell each other me and uncle Marcelo's wife that; we would see each other again, and by then I would be all grown up, ten years from our departure to Europe date, and how we would miss each other so much. Meanwhile; each day became a countdown; from the moment we moved to uncle Marcelo's house.

At the airport I walked through the immigration twice, they saw me but no body stopped me, and each time I did, I pulled my mother to follow me so that; we would go to the waiting area before boarding our plane once it was ready to start taking in it passengers. "Mãmã! Vamos tá spera ou qué, vamos passa ja. (What are you waiting for mother! Let's go pass now.)"; I said this over and over to my mother, with my most inpatient and excitement tone of voice of authority, and Lelo was a little worried; he felt that he had to tell me "Para de dar bandeira (Stop making it obvious)"; because we were getting, precisely running away. It; was important that we kept a very low profile at all times. Our name alone was; an already high profile name for the case but, for some reason I truly had my way; if I wanted and; there was no one to stop me I would have walked through everybody and straight into the plane. 'What a shame we have to go through the checking process"; I told myself every times, but I also understood that; the circumstances were different and I was not in my house.

I was like a little queen, what I ordered was done, I felt well cared for and respected, although I skipped the checking queue twice;

The first time I did; I looked straight in the face of the checking point lady, then looked straight ahead of me where I wanted and, thought I was heading to and, I impatiently did not think that; waiting is for me so, I continued walking, she did not stop me, and security did not stop me either or said anything but; my mother... She did... And, I still did not join the queue.

The second time I passed through, I passed without caring to acknowledge the lady at the checking, securities, even the policeman's working at the airport, or any other important and less important official that might had been spying on us, there were also some army man from my father's squad; but I did not care I was just too excited to had cared because; I felt so important; with mother calling my name in whisper, that I did not care of and, I went off passing through. And, went back to my mother when I felt like; she was taking long at the queue and, I wanted to tell her that also; however I ended up dragging her out of the queue with me. I wanted to show her that there was free way for us, as I managed to drag her through the checking point, security and everything else I was even more excited and loud "Olha mama! Vamos Vamos. Passa já (Mother look! Let's go let's go. Pass now)"; I told my mum with full of excitement. "Lucianna, lets go back now we need to have our passport and visa checked, and stamped from here first before we arrive in France, plus we need to show our tickets before we board on the plane if you want to board to Europe, do you?"; "if we do not follow through with the procedure we; will not be allowed go out at the airport in France we will be sent back to Angola is this what you want?"; my mom she told me with a very calm but, also worrying voice. I could sense that she was hoping that the family was not noticed by; any army, or police officials present at the airport who were not there; as my father's friend or; to watch over us while we were on the move of escaping out of the country. I sensed her worry so, I quietly and obediently walked back with my mother, Lelo was in the queue with Benjamin, and standing up and, queuing up felt like; it was time wasting and, it was very unbearable for me.

The third; time I passed through, I did it properly, with my mother and siblings, but I also was very close to breeze through especially; to avoid feeling of having to give a satisfactory conversation for permission to leave the country; as if my future actually depended on strangers...

Sleepless, and not hungry; all I wanted was to play with my doll that had stayed behind at my auntie's house with her in Mabor, Luanda not too far from the first house we lived in since mother and father got married in Russia and, moved to the country where I was born; as soon as mother had completed her university degree academic year 'I miss my doll'; I whished to had taken it with me. That; was the house in which; I received my first death threat with mother while we were in the house in that house; I was just few months old and too young to die. Mother, Lelo and I were in the house alone, as mother was bathing me in the bathroom a straight bullet fell through the ceiling of the bathroom directed to the house landed exactly in the bathroom where my mother was bathing me. My; mother was standing up and lifting me from the baby's bath basin, and as soon as we were up the straight bullet had pass through exactly where our heads were; making a hole in the ceiling and my baby bath basin then; lingered on the cemented floor of the bathroom. Lelo was seated in the living room alone not knowing that he was he almost lost his mother and little sister under the same roof of the house he was in also. It was strange, there was no conflict happening outside around the area, and no gunshots sound where made and heard, it was a day like many others as, the town and the neighbouring surrounding environment was calm and quiet. Mother thanked GOD, and three years later this death threat was followed by another death threat. A; car accident that could have taken our lives, with my dad driving his old Mazda but all thanks to GOD the accident did not happen. When I was younger I thought that they were just incidents, but now I know that GOD saved us for His purpose, He was not done with us, and He had not even started my story then, but those incidents were part of the journey my life.

I went to the toilet once during; the aeroplane journey to France out of boredom; but before I stepped in the toilet I thought that; the toilet was going to be big and specious... 'Oh dear!' To my disappointment. I attempted to wee by force not to turn my journey to the toilet to a waste of time but, nothing would come out, and I felt like 'yak'; I did not want to touch or, let anything touch me. However; I flashed to see if it would really flash as, everything looked tacky and not to be working to me, and I soon after went out back to my seat; and again the white tall man with blond hair was looking at me and smiling. I walked straight to my seat and sat down without saying a word pretending not to have seen the man smiling to me. Looking around; it seemed as thou almost everyone was a sleep, but I could not get a sleep, and so it went on for many weeks after we arrived in Paris, France. One minute I wanted to seat at one of the window seats to look outside the window; I wanted to see the clouds and; almost touch them too, as I also; knew that the windows could not be opened, and the next minute I wanted to remain were I had sat, high above in front of me was a television, and I wanted to watch it; I was curious as to what program would have come on the aeroplane television especially; that late at nigh. Things were running through my mind, but I hoped that; whatever program they'd put on was going to be good for children.

However; nothing suitable for my age came on.

We; landed in Paris in the morning hours after leaving Luanda in the afternoon; while many people call jet lag, I did not know;

what I felt, and all I recall was that; I was still very excited to have relocated at last! 'I had gotten on the plane, and now I am in another country, in Paris, France! The city of chick, 'Europe here I am''. I thought that the fashion lifestyle that Paris represented fitted well for my mother type of person; her character, personality and her likes; chick, elegant, and very nice ladies. Lucianna was glad that they still had money.

Lucianna had seen around Chinese people before in her country, but almost every foreign passenger she saw at the Paris, France airport was Chinese, or Japanese? She could not tell the difference between the two nationalities. Before; the family reach the pick up area of the airport; there was a long queue in the ladies restroom area waiting to get into the WC as soon as she entered the ladies restroom; to use the ladies WC Lucianna was shocked to know that; the long queue she had seen from far away was for the ladies WC. Again; to her surprise, there was only Chinese or Japanese woman waiting on the queue, walking in and out of the toilets, and she was the only child and the only black person there waiting to use the WC. She remembers of how most of the women were looking at her; mesmerised and she had started thinking that; maybe they had never seen a black person before! But; Lucianna did not care neither did she feel scared, but she felt very shy. At the same time those ladies looked as though; they were very enchanted, and they smiled at Lucianna which; then she felt as though 'It's not a bad thing; that they were looking at me because; maybe they also liked me despite the fact that I was different from them'; the long faces suddenly looked brightened at seeing a little girl, who was so shy but filled with life and guts more then maybe most woman that; were waiting on the queue. She wanted to asked one of the Chinese lady who was; queuing up if the queue was for the toilet, but "I couldn't, I did not know what language she spoke other then Chinese that I also; spoke"; however it was quickly confirmed that; she did not speak French, or a language that Lucianna could speak or understand; as she dropped few French words in attempt to make a phrase to ask the question, and in response she replied in Chinese; by her facial expression as Lucianna recalls; she looked confused as if she did not understand a word of what Lucianna had spoken. Lucianna already spoke a little bit of French and; also understood the language a little bit, but it was not enough to have engaged in a conversation with another child or with anyone at all; and in some occasions the harder she tried to perfect her French it was the more she was made fun of, leaving her feeling knocked down.

Living in Paris was hard for Lucianna, out of everyone amongst her family; her mother already spoke fluent French, Lelo spoke better French the her and easily mixed with the other kids, Benjamin was still a baby, and most of her times were spent playing with him then other kids.

The grown ups accepted and loved her so much; they found her to be a very beautiful girl, she was always being complimented by strangers, and the neighbours they had in the different places they'd lived. Julianna had heard never-ending congratulations on her children about their education, disciplinary level and their beauties; and Lucianna's beauty was always appreciated and the most talked about by every adult, whilst Lelo's beauty was very much appreciated by the ladies. However; for Lucianna it was a different story when it came to other children

Bullied, names called at her, alienated, and made fun of for being black especially because; she was the only little black girl and African in their neighbourhood and, made fun of for not speaking French well at first, but she was learning the language while she listened to other children speak in conversation. On occasions the other girls would try to fight her, or pull her hair.

It was strange to be in a neighbourhood covered with white tenants, although they were; a few black French families scattered in the town; when the white adults were polite, gentle and kind with one another and to children. I saw white children, being

60

nice and respectful to white children, but the white girls bullied and only pushed away black girls, or did not acknowledge them at all, especially me. I saw and felt no sympathy from those children; except from Louisa a French girl, born of Portuguese parents. Me, and her were close, she was always happy to see me and always wanted to play with me especially, her parents and her grandma. We, had few things in common; we both spoke Portuguese, she liked to smile like; I also liked to smile, she was the first friend I had who's invited me to dinner in her house and meet her family; but I said I can't; as I preferred that her parents had asked my mother first, and after all I did. The; first time Louisa's mother saw me, she told me "Awww you are so beautiful...! Louisa is always talking about you at home, her grandmother too"; I smiled and said thank you ma'am. The other white girls used to be jealous of our friendship, and the hated me even more; they didn't want me around despite my attempts to be friend with them. If Louisa was not there and, I had gone around to play outside with the other girls, it always resulted to a sad story for me; I either ran back home at my grand aunts house where we spent our last moment together as a family before; I was left behind retrieved in a foyer, and before reunited with my family in the UK; crying or arriving in the house and begging my mother to play with me for a while. Which; it also never happened. Shopping was my comfort; as it was easy to reach boutiques, department store, and grocery store, and I from a young age already had a love and passion for fashion. I was always ought to find chick dress code; the Parisian style for my mother, and for me too; at times I used to whish I was all grown up so that I would be able to try on some of the chic clothes I saw in the luxury and designers boutiques. I used to hide in between all the chic cloth fantasising to have all the best in the world, after all my family has been through. I never stopped hoping (looking up to the clouds).

After Lucianna's mother and sibling all entered to the UK, Lucianna was always lonely; she no longer had Louisa in her life, and met a whole lot of new people which; she then had to coexist with new strangers, infants, children and adolescents both orphans, abandoned, and mal self ported children; they were also children which; their parents had lost custody battle, and by the courts order they were taken away and over to the French authority and social services care. Each child had a personal judge and lawyer.

Lucianna spent a lot of her time shopping; she wanted a life and, so she found it in satisfying her need; a doll, toys and Barbie, clothes and shoes, and her mother did her hair. However; when she lived at the foyer she did not do much of the stuff she was habituated to be doing with her mum, and family.

The white boys were kind to me; although we did not play together and, not spoken to each other when we walked past each other each with our parent; but there a silent greet that only the eyes knew of 'I know you'. They got along with the black children altogether if they were to spend time together by coexistence in public places such; as the park, or school playground. Children who came from, and were brought up to be racist were never actually racist themselves whenever; they did anything that showed they racism it was due to the pressure they faced at home from hearing the horrible words which convey racism. I think my mother knew of what I was going through socially, as I was the only child of hers that she always did not allow to go out, and stopped my thoughts of being friends with the other children; it almost felt like she meant 'they are not good enough to be your friend'; this is what Lelo and I went through; back in the home land. Overly protective parents for different reasons, but it had continued, it did not stop there.

Me, and my mom at home together everyday; knowing fully well that we were not as close as; I always wanted to be with mother and longed for, there was always a huge gap of disconnection between us. It used to pain me; I wished and wanted more from my mother; the closeness of mother and daughter, like;

she was with Lelo; considering that Julianna had always left me out of everything and anything, and it always led me to believe that I was only good for cleaning and tidying the house, clean after my siblings and learn how to cook; as a hand full of help only. For Lucianna a must learn how to cook was mandatory because; she is a female, and to be growing up catering to her father and her brothers was always the major exam especially for her cooking skills. Julianna also; put Lucianna to be catering for her stepsister Essa who actually knows how to do nothing, when Lucianna was at the age that; Essa is now Lucianna had already started doing house chore, and cooking at times for the family. Julianna always made sure that; Lucianna never got away from it.

"Most times I felt like; she really truly hated me, and cared not, and that maybe was also the reason for our major disconnection"; says Lucianna.

Her actions often; showed that she definitely preferred her sons and, stepdaughter as to her own daughter "I had many reasons and still do to believe so"; Lucianna painfully remembers of how she felt that; she was being turned into the stepchild and the outsider of the family, the daughter of a rival.

Julienna at times thinks that; her daughter is meant to be at the service of everyone she wants and do what she as the mother is supposed to do; letting Lucianna feel the heavy weight responsibility of motherhood before her time, siblings, including stepsister, and her father, "Oh! Extended family too, at times when they come around"; but Lucianna refuses to subject her-self as so, 'is too much! I have to be me in my time'. Everyone has to take care of his or hers own responsibility for a healthy balance.

"There is nothing wrong with helping and taking responsibility; as a daughter, sister, niece, or cousin; but the boundaries are crossed all the times"; Lucianna feels happy with herself, for being a good sister and daughter, also as a result she can and, knows how to do the house chores especially cook as; she likes her cooking, but when boundaries are crossed principals are also, broken.

During Lucianna's live in Paris; she felt very little close to her mother but, much more unified as; she had seen that her mother became; a little aware of her daughter. Lucianna imagined that; the distant closeness between her and Julianna was; due to the circumstances of relocation, and her thinking about the long distance between her and her husband, including his problem etc. There were times that; the little nine years old Lucianna made her mother even more worried; the thought of running away sometimes used to come to her mind, but this time around alone, without her Lelo her big brother. She seemingly grew inpatient of waiting for her mother to come around, and look at her as her daughter, and let her see her kindness, and motherly love for Lucianna. A conversation about anything would have been enough for Lucianna to feel that she was cared about, or just a listening ear from Julianna. Sooner she ran way; she was gone for many hours of the day, she had breakfast with her sibling and after a while; she went out of the house without telling anyone, and she hid herself throughout the whole day as, she was worried that someone saw her and took back to her mother. However; Lucianna got tired of hiding in the park and the corners of the street, and started walking in the open street wandering around; and when she got tired she found a bench right next to the flat they were living which, was opposite the supper market her mother did most of their grocery shopping course. She saw her brother Lelo wondering outside looking for her everywhere but; she did not move an inch close to him, she wanted to be invisible, as she did not want to be found. And, earlier in the day she also saw her mother with all her siblings looking for her; she just knew that they were looking for her. But; she did not want to go them, she wanted to be left alone, she was tired of being set off all the time, at that very moment she did not like anyone in her family.

Finally; Lucianna returns back to the house alone in the latest of the afternoon of the same day; she was really tired, and she also knew that; by going back home before she is let to take a bath, have snack, or maybe dinner or just fall straight to seep, and while at it; her mother would had told her off for disappearing all throughout the day; especially unresponsive to their search for her.

"Where were you? We have been looking for you. Lucianna what happened? Mother has been very worried about you, she will get angry when; she'll see you watch"; Lelo tells' Lucianna at the elevator door way, as he was about to go outside to look for his sister one more time however; Lucianna did not expect anything less.

Into; the house they entered, and her heart furious, and speedily sinking down to her stomach "Voce foste aonde? Huh? (Where did you go? Huh?)"; standing at the door, as soon as Julianna saw her that was it. She was not going to smack her daughter, but Lucianna was also not worried of any punished, and she was also not looking forward anything, she was not even sure if; she was going to return to the house.

Her family were there with her for only a short while of six months during; the time she was far away from her family Lucianna was; able and had time to think about her dreams as a kid, and of how she would achieve her dreams. Her dream had not changed but; the vision she first had when she was in her country of how to achieve her dream had changed immensely. When she was a much younger kid she wanted to have a career in the oil industry of Angola, she loved the idea of working in a man power dominated industry and facing the challenges; but making the difference and more money then the man. Back then; men were mostly the people who worked in the oil industry in her thoughts, but Lucianna was determined to be there. The change of culture, country, climate, she not being even sure, nor knowing where her parents were, and of the continent and country they would finally settle in, made things change for her on how to achieve her dreams and ambitions. She did not know, and lucked guidance. But; Lucianna discovered her passion for fashion design when she was in Paris when; she was in the foyer when she met a specific supposedly; fourteen years old teenager, as she looked like she was nineteen years of age and over.

"Once in my grand aunt's house, I heard that there were many Africans who left their homeland and on arrival in Europe they changed their names, age completely, to add on pressure to be accepted and given the right to stay and to remain in the country the younger you are in age the better, and of course in combination with their immigration story", "I used to think 'How appalling'; a 40 years old man would become a fourteen years old boy"; as for the Arabs it was a story of identity, and Lucianna never understood how they always escaped.

The girls used to like to draw female figure with fashion clothes on, and I like her drawing and I wanted to further my drawing skills, and she had taught me how; and the easiest way to draw a shirt on the bodice with elephant legs shaped jeans which; is a timeless fashion French. But; Lucianna learned with her mother how to draw couture dresses of the Victorian era, skirts, tops and blouses. During; that time there was a Brazilian drama novella that; came on called 'Chica Da Silva'; it was about a black slave the first to had had been a lover of a rich and powerful white man who, then became her master... It was a very captivating novella, everyone including children loved it, and I loved the fashion "Couture it is"; my mother told me, and little did I know. The first; time she drew them alone without her mother's supervision she designed clothes for her favourite Barbie although she preferred to play with power ranger.

Living 'Chez les Moyen, dens le foyer'; each individual child had his and hers own caseworker who would also a one of the carers; some carers were very rude, and personal faith in GOD and religion was not tolerated in the place, children were not allowed to be heard saying that GOD exists, especially not be caught praying. My mother always told me that GOD listens to children; and I in that place alone without formal communication, I did not know if I was ever going to see my brothers Lelo, Uche and Benjamin especially my father and mother. There were times that I prayed every day and night for a miracle; my mother's family who live in Paris, France and else where in the French provinces; knew of what had happened to me, and their presence was required for them to take me back with them, it. I was told three days

"We have contacted your grand aunt and she has been notified that you are here and she said she will come to pick you up tomorrow"; the social care service workers told me.

"For; the three days this was the news update I heard that; came from my mother's family in France. It was always tomorrow, but tomorrow never came"; I was saddened, shocked and disappointed, but it did not sudden me as much, as I personally had no emotion attachment to any of them, I never heard of them or saw them growing up, and nor did I feel as welcomed in their homes, it all seemed to be out of interest from their end and, not genuinely out of the love and worry. Except; from a cousin of my father and her husband, in their house I felt as though I as well as, my mother, brothers and sister were welcome. They opened the doors of their houses to us and, mother was thankful.

I wanted mother, I wanted to play with my siblings, I had missed my father; but I could not, till my family here in the UK had received their indefinite stay to remain in the United Kingdom. And; thank GOD I was granted my visa to enter and rejoin my family in the UK; as my family case was very critical, and serious. The authorities in the United Kingdom treated it with much investigation in search of the truth, and the French authority that had custody of me also, remained waiting and worried in case the United Kingdom refused to take us in and offer refuge to us. I had told them what was happening, and that we were desperate for international refuge and, protection.

After; one year of wait, legal fight, and in depth investigation, the authorities confirmed who we were, where we came from, and why we had come to them. It; was confirmed and known that, the truth is what was told and so I later given the green light to enter into the United Kingdom.

The foyer was open to give me up for adoption after the three days had passed; to any family who wanted me in theirs, and I was never going to see my family again.

After; three months she shows up at the foyer to visit me for the first time; my grand aunt... she told me that she had been at work that is why she could not come to pick me up or visit me earlier, and I wondered why didn't someone else from the family come to pick me up and take me to her house, if I was still accepted to stay there since her husband's doing were out in the open. I had told them who was responsible and held my passport, and the foyer recovered my passport and kept it safely in the foyer locked in the chairman's office. "I feel very grateful to the foyer because; they cared and took good care of me"; my personal care and the care worker was always there for me; when I was sad, happy, when I needed to ask questions, she was there to answer them if she could answer, she made things smooth for me, made sure I did not fall a victim in the hands of other kids and adults by maltreatment too.

By; the time she came to visit me, I spoke better French and I was already a fluent French speaker, I understood it very well, I had also become adapted to the foyer rules, the other kids and all the stuff. I met many children, and I was always blackmailed by the girl who taught me how to draw female shirts and the jeans, after my lawyer found my mother and siblings with all the information, and description of them and the family I come from in general, my legal team departed on the journey to keep contacts with mother, and know how she was doing. I remember how excite my lawyer was to break the new to my personal carer and caseworker; as soon as; Elisa received the news, she

68

was so happy and excited for me "Tu vá parlé au telephone avec ta maman, au na trouver elle et tes frère et ta seur (We have found your mother, and you brothers and sister! You will speak with your mother on the telephone"; when Elisa broke this news to me I was astonished and very happy that they found my family for me. The power of GOD was the reason behind that great news, the development of everything; including the support Elisa gave me and put on my case. She pushed forward for that, she used to tell me "I know is being very hard for you"; and at times she told me "something is missing from your smile"; I heard her talking with her colleagues in the Moyen corridor. Elisa used to sound very worried, and I used to pass by pretending I did not hear her. She was blond, not tall, and she wore glasses, she was good to all the children.

Every carer was different, some kind, some arrogant, and a few bullies; Lucianna remembers once they were taken out to a park of attraction, and on entering into the park her shoes laces got untied Lucianna went down to tie up her shoes laces, as she was down Murray a male care walked straight toward Lucianna and, gave her very hard cu de pie (fly kicked) her bum; however; it was not the bum he intended to kick and nor did he kick her bum. Murray had kicked Lucianna's private external genitalia part "Ay"; she screamed.

"I screamed, and looked behind me to see who had kicked me and why? And saw it was Murray, his facial expression showed and said it all; and his unapologetic response to me made me feel violated and victimised"

I did not enjoy the rest of my trip, I was always conscious of his presence; and I could not understand why was that that man done such to me. I was physically hurt, and I became shy, I could not speak with the others, and while socialising I was quiet. The night was horrible for me. I could not stop thinking what had happened "What? Who are you looking at? I will do it again, shame on you hahahaaa"; that was his response. In the morning; Elisa heard about it from him recounting what he had done with laughter and his face amused in the office, but Elisa was not happy and did not find it to be amusing either. I could hear from my bedroom her voice and the exchange of words, and at six o'clock in the morning just as I was getting up; Elisa opens the door of my bedroom and asks me of how I was, by the next day I was pain free, and became disgusted at Murray, when I saw him I greeted him, just like; my mother taught me, to do when I see or meet people; to greet first. I minded my own business, I hardly ever was close to him, and he was there to take care of us.

There were swings, slides, and basketball basket; we played out in the playground three times a day, it was a routine and rules that by; six in the evening we were not allowed to be anywhere else but in les Moyen. At first; I was excited that there was a mini park at our disposal; in the playground, but with the passing of time it became boring and, suffocating as that; was our only fresh air. Outside was the main road; for us to see the activities that happened outside, we had to be up in les Moyen's balcony, as the walls and gate were so high and not see through.

Children from all over the world origin, came, stayed and left; they found me there and left me there, for some children they got adopted by a family very fast within their first day stay in les Moyen, for others; it was the case of their judge's decision to send them back home to their parents and hope they'd behave, and be good children, some children were there because their parent or parents could not afford to bring them up. Like; Ama and her little brother, they were only one year apart in age; but their mother could not take care of them, she once told me that their father abandoned her with her children and never wanted anything with them, and she was struggling alone; she was a very beautiful Moroccan lady. I felt sorry for her, and I asked what about her family, instead of living her children in that place, that restricted her from seeing them. She; was only allowed to see them three time a week although; they were well treated to what I saw. She cried, and she did not answer me all that she said was "You are still a child, you won't understand. Don't worry"; every time I saw her, she always looked down, I saw volumes of falling tears in her. She was going through the silent suffering alone.

Later on I met Daly and Simba they were both Congolese girls, who came also in the foyer; when I met them especially Simba; we were both really happy and enchanted to have met. We became friends straight away although; it took a little more of my part for her to feel more welcome, as I knew what it was like to suddenly move from a place where you as child know everyone to another new place; that you did not know anything of, and your family is distances away. How you miss them or want to go to were they are; is unexplainable but; rather read from your daily facial expression, your character, attitude, body language, and most of all silence. She was very silent; I felt I had to be loud for her to distract herself from her thoughts of sadness, hurt, and disappointment from her foster parents or even parents who gave her up to foster family. I did not know the real reason as to how she ended up in the hands of the French government social care; all I knew was that there was some sort of involvement of foster care in her case. Simba and I had the same carer and caseworker Elisa; she introduced us to each other, and told us go chat away! "Lucianna I have a friend for you"; she told me with excitement. Not long after we would chill outside in the play ground, while I felt so comfortable laying down on the ground and stair into the blue bright sky of spring, deep into the clouds. It felt good but it used to bring impatience to me, because; I would then want to sit on my mother's lap, as though I did when I was an infant. Simba would caress Lucianna's head "it's okay" she used to say. With Elisa I could always see and feel her humble heart and positive will which; always stroke me as, 'she likes; her job, and she is a carer out of love and passion to care for other, especially for children who were not even her actual biological children'; I looked up to her. With; time I got used to my situation, but it was always painful and hard to live in that reality. And; Simba Simba was really kind to me, the only girl that had been my friend, and kind to me after Louisa, she listened to me, and she became my buddy every time I played at the playground, when we played hide and seek as a group, and on Thursdays movie night we usually walked into the theatre room together although; we did not always sit next to one another. Simba was more timid then I, and Daly was a very loud girl, she was always in trouble she argued with all the boys, and debated against the carers, including her personal judge. Every time they came back from court, to hear her judge's decision on something her carer always came back worn out with bad news. 'Her mouth really got her punished by the judge's order'.

But; soon they both had left the foyer, and again I was left wondering 'when would my turn come?' I felt very lonely, all the kids I knew were all gone, and there were not as many kids left in the foyer anymore except from the babies, their ward was always full of them.

At that point I felt short and, I did not know what else to ask GOD in prayer I felt like; HE was never receiving my prayers, I could not bring myself to think of what was going on with my family in the United Kingdom either; because they were too far. "I didn't want to think"; it was emotionally draining and mentally torturing to me. Stayed quiet; and calm, as; each day past by I became more and more sad because; I felt lonely, and I was not certain that I was going to meet my mom and siblings again; I was emotionally trapped; crying in the inside but smiling in the outside. Smiling suddenly became a heavy task for me, and my only consolation was that 'At least I will speak to them on the phone on wednesday'; my mother's first word on the telephone to me; the first time she called after they had finally traced her was "I love you my daughter; "I have never forgotten you, I did not abandon you, I looked for you every where, paid lawyers to help with the search but nobody found you, but I never gave up"; my grand aunt did not even tell her niece where; her daughter of nine years old was, and not even a contact details was passed on to my mother, since no word was spoken of my where about. I went to school in the foyer, and in the last six months of my stay there, I received no visitor I did not go outside of the foyer. For; the times that I did I went in the van and straight to the Marie De Paris sports centre to practice sport but that; was before Simba arrived at the foyer.

We were also; taken to many holidays activity camp, ski, given horse back riding lessons, camping; but most of all we practiced a lot of sports, and each child had the opportunity to choose the sport of their choice to practice in the national level, almost like; a career starter it was fun; and it took my mind away from my problems. Christmas was always great, every child received multiple presents, and on Easter we played Easter game with the Easter chocolate rabbits, and every child always wanted to find the biggest of them all.

I stopped watching time and suddenly; in a morning I was unexpectedly served with the news that; my family had finally received the indefinite stay to remain in the United Kingdom, and that the Mr at the United Kingdom embassy in Paris, France was awaiting for my visit to give me my visa to rejoin my family. My heart exploded of joy; I started to count the days after my interview at the embassy. And; one day Elisa entered in les Moyen with my passport in her hand with the biggest smile walking towards me, through the double doors of the les Moyen, and (Boom!) she shouted "you now have your visa! You are going to the United Kingdom to join your family!!!!"; I smiled, and from that moment I became certain that, I was going to see my mum, siblings and dad again 'Once more I will be with them'; I couldn't stop trying to imagine how Lelo must have grown up by then, Uche, Benjamin and Essa too. I was happy, I could not wait to meet Lelo my big brother again, and I had missed my dad so much. With; this news, I pray in me to thank GOD for the miracle, everyone believed it was a miracle that; I returned to my family, that things happened the way they did because; it could have been a lot worst, but it was not worst because; GOD had put the pieces of the puzzle together for me.

Elisa started to explain to me the procedure of my travel journey; she wanted to be the one to bring me to the United Kingdom to my family, but it was decided that; my lawyer Madame Bartholomew was going to bring me home on the Eurostar train from Paris Gar De Nort to London St Pancras international. And so we made the journey from Paris to London on a Wednesday morning and we arrived in London in the afternoon. Waiting for my arrival at the station was my father and Lelo; Lelo and I ran toward each other, and we both hugged when we met across and that; was the most heart felt hug I had ever received in my life; it came from my big brother excluding my parent's affection.

But; I also did not forget the foyer; it was too soon, and I had already started thinking about going back one day to visit them; everyone although; the rest of the children I left in there; that I met would have been gone too by then, and there would only be new faces, I looked forward visiting the carers and my last hope is that they would still be there and remember me. Lucianna left les Moyen, Paris, France with a little multi colour notebook where she had written the contacts of the other children before they left the foyer for; contacts purposes. We wanted; to stay in touch, and talk to each other although; they knew that there was a great possibility that I was going to rejoin my family in the United Kingdom and we would never cross paths in the street of Boulevard, Paris or le quartorzièm, Paris when; we become adults unless we kept in touch; there was a fear of forgetness amongst us the kids; for some of us we were each the only family of each other, and we individual felt uncertainty of our future. It was the more reason why we exchanged our contact details amongst ourselves. Unfortunately; for me I had no address or, a telephone number to give. I did not know where my family where, and after I found them, their address and telephone number was not permanent, nor did I held any of their old contact details, the office had it in my file. Therefore; I could only take the telephone numbers and addresses of some of the children's family home and direct cell phone number of some children, who already had a cell phone outside of the foyer. Inside the foyer we had no right and, must have never be seen with cell phone; for the children who could; they went back to their family homes for the weekends only I took their contact details; and for those who could not, we stayed inside everyday till it was time to leave the foyer and move on to a foster family, adoptive parents, another foyer, or back to their family if it was ruled by the personal judge.

For Lucianna rejoining her family was; what she wanted, but had forgotten what was like to live with and within her family life, she was confused; and it later became unpleasing. Her father being a bad character and examples to her, and his despise for to her mother brother really bothered her; sometimes she felt like going back to the foyer, or if the people she met at the foyer felt like; he was a genuine and self-respected character.

"Ton père se ressembler un prèsident! (Your father looks like the president of a country)"; the carers used to tell Lucianna when they saw his picture, and she used to tell him during their telephone conversations what people were saying about him when they saw his picture. His reaction was always exciting and so; happy to hear it, Madame Bartholomew had also told Malto when she took Lucianna to London, United Kingdom to join her family, and everyday Malto said it in the hotel apartment that the family was living that; he looked young and he looked like a president and everybody liked him.

He used to tell my mother that; she will get old, ugly and wrinkly before him, and he still looked young, and she looked old and more tired then him and tired. Most; of the times that he made those rude, blind, untrue and very insulting remarks about mother's physical appearance was in front of all of us, especially me; many at times I thought that, he used to do that, to diminish mother's self esteem, and I was right. The worst times were the late hours of the night moving on to the early hours of the morning before; I went to bed, as I was struggling with adapting to the time difference, the house, and being part of a family again. I slept very late at four o'clock in the morning for most days; I was usually the only person awake with my dad keeping me company. I started to feel noxious and nervous after my second night back with my family; the first night we did a sleepover camping in the middle of the leaving room, we chatted together till we fell asleep... With me being the last person to fall asleep.

Reality of life in Lucianna's family started to sink in from the second night she was settled in with her family; Lucianna was up till late, seated on the royal blue with orange diamond repeated pattern chair looking through; an English language learning paperwork and trying to do reading with a Portuguese and English dictionary, and a French and English dictionary on the table. They were Lelo's English paperwork he gave them to me; to help me with the first stages of learning English, they were what helped him with adapting with the English language and speaking it before; he even had started going to school; Julianna also; had similar one. My mother used to tell me, that they were good to learn English and help me form the main and basic words, and to form phrases or, questions of day to day life, and then it would not be so hard for me to communicate and understand a little bit the language once I started to go to school. Lelo started speaking English fluently in one week after of living in the United Kingdom; thanks to the free English classes he took on arrival, where the English language learning paperwork were given to him. When mother arrived in the UK apart from; my mother's personal interpreter; who was present with my mother in important appointments and meetings; Lelo was the person who helped mother with her English. During; those first stages of living in the United Kingdom Lelo was a father to Uche, Benjamin and Essa, and the men of the house helping mother with everything which; Malto never helped her with, and ironically he still is like; a father to us; he took care of Uche and Benjamin when mother could not because she had to attend important appointments, and when she was out of the house, Lelo cooked if there was no prepared cooked food, for them when Uche, Benjamin and Essa where hungry, he bathed them, he changed Uche's and Benjamin's nappies, he helped them to read children's book; even though they were too small to understand anything but; Lelo used to do that so, that they can get used to hearing and feel natural to adapting to a new environment and the different language, and also that; growing and speaking English would be natural for them. Lelo used to help do the grocery shopping for mum, he would walk forty-five minutes from the hotel to the most affordable grocery supermarket store which; was also the closest to the hotel to buy six bottles of water, and whatever; was missing and mother needed to cook a meal at home, and he walked back home for forty-five minutes with the shoppings. He also; cleaned, fix broken things including the electrical apparel equipment and its maintenances even after Malto arrived in the United Kingdom and, came to live with the family meanwhile; Malto did nothing to help neither his wife nor children. Lelo became his slave, but he also pulled back from helping as much as he did when; my dad was not there

"Não mãmã I'm not going to help you with picking up my brothers from school is not my job! That's his job, I'm not the father here he is." "I'm not going I'm tired"

With so much revolt Lelo started to object to helping mom out like; he used to, and my mother understood Lelo, and she knew that he was right to want to take a back stand because; for one Lelo was just a kid and a very good kid and by that; his childhood had always been taken away, and trampled on by our father Malto. And, by him continuing to help her instead of my father, meant fully putting on adult's responsibilities on him. Lelo was just and still a kid. That; was too much, it was daily diary routine that Lelo had to do in order for the family to function properly, by helping my mother Julianna, and Malto did not care, in fact! He used to sit expecting praises from visitors who came to visit them in the hotel, and used to find Lelo always doing things, and they were things that are heavy for a kid because; they were responsibilities for a father; that he used to take care of.

"Ummm, boss tu a la chance eh! Tu est trés bien. Toi ici Lelo fait tout pour toi, même brosser tes chaussures, regardez çá? Nous les autre là chez notre maison, on droit faire tout nous-méme, on a persone pour s'occuper de prendre notre responsabilité. Ton fils a la même age que mon fils, ils sont tous infant me regard Lelo il est antre de vouz aider, mon fils il fait que jouer tout le temps (Boss you are lucky! You are perfectly fine. Up here Lelo does everything for you; even down to brushing your shoes just look at that? For the rest of us at home we have to do everything ourselves, we don't have anyone to take care of our responsibilities. Your son has the same age as my son, they are all children, but look at your son he is helping you, all my son does is play all the time)"

When I had arrived to join the family; we were still living in the hotel, and an uncle came to visit us, and these was one of the things he said to my dad during; his visit after seeing Lelo as, busy as he was and he seemed mesmerised; sounding as though he wished that Lelo was his son, so that he would rest from his responsibilities for his son to take care of it whilst he sat on his buttocks like; my father doing nothing only relaxing and enjoying that he had slaves. He was also; comparing my brother to his son and seeing nothing wrong with what he saw. "A mentality of one who is in Africa, with a backward mind"; I told my self when I heard the uncle speaking like that. I saw it to be very negative, that adults saw that; it is positive for a child to take care of adult's responsibility, and I instantly felt sorry for my brother. I did not like; what my uncle was saying so; I left the living room and went to the bedroom I was sharing with my three siblings, and sometimes four siblings.

Once again; as many other times; Lucianna started having a flashback of the time she was still living in the foyer, and she wanted to be with her family, the times that she felt like; crying because; she had missed them and she was scared and uncertain if she was ever going to see them again. And; she thought to herself 'What is the difference between my carers there and my parents?'; the eleven years old young girl felt confused. Every day after midnight hour as, she stayed up late her father would also always be there. "Essa tua mãe é uma burra, idiota, não tenh nada na cabeça (Your mother is dumb idiot, she has nothing in her head)"; my father told me those words every single day and every time my mother was not at home or when she was asleep; just as, everyone else. I understood that; he only used to stay up late with me every night to talk about my mother behind her back, and insult her.

Lucianna was shocked; and totally confused speechless without answers, and input to his gossiping initiation about her mother. These were the only conversation he ever brought up; Lucianna was filled with dislike; toward her father as, he backstabbed her mother, and gossiped to her, and called her mother bad names. Lucianna always thought of her mother to be very and highly intelligent; but in the presence of her father she felt frightened to stand up for her mother, and often pretended as if the things he said were not hurting or angering her. She did not want to hear them, and she did not want Malto to be there with her whenever she was alone, especially if Julianna was not there present 'So are those things also what he tells my siblings; when mother isn't present?'; Lucianna wondered and strove never to be left alone with him.

"Hoje vamos mas conversa ya sobre aquilo, não esqueçe (we will talk about it again today, do not forget)"; when he woke up before he went out he reminded Lucianna of the conversation he stuffed her head with and conspired against her mother while; he tried to bring Lucianna on board.

He spoke as, if he had a much more damaging plan against Julianna, he spoke as if he wanted Lucianna to come to hate, disregard, disrespect and, feel embarrassed of her mother.

"Isso è nosso segredo, não fala na tua mãe ta ouvir? Se voçe falar, vas ver ou que vou te fazer; bom eu vou já ta? Chao (This is our secret, do not tell your mother did you hear ma? If you do tell her, you will see what I will do to you okay? Bye)"

I was very intimidated but; the more he did that the more disgusted at him I was, and the more I did not want to sit with him and have a conversation with him about anything, as that implied having grown up conversations, like grown ups and he would always escalate everything for negativity. However; his impulsion at what he was doing, and his threats, opened my eyes to reality, 'he was never an upright man in heart'; my moral instinct of right and wrong encouraged me to stand for what was right.

On a morning; after this had been happening for some days after Lucianna rejoined the family in the hotel, Lucianna waited for Malto to go out, as he always did in the afternoon, although it was not to work. She could not wait till she told her mum, and the words that her dad had said were so vivid in her mind and, very disturbing to her that all she wanted was to get it out of her and let her mother know of the thing being said behind her back; which saddened her very much. She did not want be stuck in between her parents if; they were having problems; she did not want to be guilty of innocence again "Se eu mori meu sangue ya cair na tua cabeça (If I had died my blood would have fallen on your head)"; Lucianna always remembered the conversation she and her mother had long time ago when; they were living in Paris altogether, and her mother explained why certain things happened between her and her father when they were still in Luanda, and their consequences. Her father was having many affairs with many different women behind her mother's back, but there was a specific woman who triggered Julianna. Once;

he took Lucianna to a women's house, and when they arrived at the house "the women offered me food and drinks, but I said no thank you ma'am". As, "My mother taught me not to be accepting food or drink, and be nosy as well as, noisy in other people's house especially strangers; but the moral was to have good manners"; as soon as I was excused to seat down, my father then proceeded into another room of the house walking behind that woman. I sat alone quietly, but I could not understand what was going on, and why did my dad go into a room with another women in her house; and closed the door behind him. I was very curious, once he came out of that room, that women was behind him; and still not word from either of them 'is father being unfaithful to my mother? And who is this woman?'; I asked myself. I also asked my father in the car about what was he doing in that room, and why did we go to her house, but he answered me not, so I stayed silent. I was felt like; he was having an affair with her. It; was around ten o'clock at night, when we arrived home and my mother hadn't seen much of me on that day. I was angry and revolted and, I made it a point to tell mother so, I told her where I went, where my father took me to that women's house, and told her that father went inside a room with that women alone and closed the door behind him, and I was left alone seating her living room sofa and everything seemed strange and unacceptable to me.

I was six and a half years old; but as usual she decided to take no notice to what I told her, anything I saw, heard and was going through my mind. It; did not matter to her because; I was not getting beaten and abused everyday like Lelo; she never had or made time for me like; she did for Lelo, and I felt it. I was a kid and I wanted to tell her many more things, but it was so hard to because she did not pay attention, but even so I did not care I said it, I needed to say everything I had heard, saw, felt and I did not hide an inch of the details. Few years later I then found out that mother found out that her husband had been having multiples affairs for years, and the women Malto took me to her house was also one of the women he had an affair with. My mother was seven months pregnant and almost died during an argument with my father about his man whore ways, she caught high blood pressure in an instant and proceeded to a heart attack. During; the argument Malto hit her, and she retaliated by; picking his army boot up that were near close to the side of their bed, to throw at him; and in the process she hit her hand on the their bed frame as, she lifted up her arms to throw the boot at him in retaliation. And; that was when she dropped on the floor, she was not moving, and she seemed to be struggling to breath, as how I found her when Lelo woke me up in the middle of that night crying. "Lucianna acorda a mãe dismaio (Lucianna wake up mother has fainted)"; he was crying, when he was telling me my mind went blank, and with out understanding what he meant by 'fainted'; just like that? I ran with Lelo to their bedroom and, I found mother on the floor unconscious. Uche was five months old, and crying for her beside where her body was laying down, it was almost like he knew that his mother was not well and it was serious. She was not waking up, and she was not moving

Uche did not stop crying, he did not want anyone to carry him but; mother

And I was very scared "Lelo Mãmã ta morta? (Lelo is mother dead?)"; I asked Lelo, and my dad was scared all he did was walk around in and out their bedroom thinking about what to do and not doing anything, but I was not concerned about him. Lelo and I watched in a movie once; a man pour cold water on the face of a woman who was down on the ground because; she had fainted. We kept on calling our mother but but; she just was not waking up, and we received no response from her. We were crying and desperately wanted to know that she was still alive and was going to be oky, and there we walled louder and louder.

Lelo filled a bucked with cold water brought into our parent's room and we both threw it on my mother's face, but she did not wake up.

While she was down and pregnant on the floor me and my brother were trying to revive her and crying for her with Uche, Malto was telling me that; it was her fault, and she was the one beating him however; Lelo had witnessed everything that happened and he had also already told me about everything. And; to Lelo he was saying

"Please forgive me, help me I promise you I will never do this again"

I knew he was lying that was typical of him, is what he does best.

That; was the more reason why I did not care about him although; I was worried, as there were thought of him possibly going to jail, if my mother had died; however I couldn't care about him. I was loosing my mother because of him.

As, scared as I was something comforted me deep inside me, and told me that she was going; to be fine, when mother woke up, she was in hospital. In Paris I asked mother what caused what happened that nigh at home, and immediately she looked and sounded heart broken, as she started to tell me why...

To my shock; she blamed me about it, she put me in the list of the people who were to be blamed and would have been responsible by divine justice; if she had died. I felt heart broken because; she told me that I wanted her to die

"Se eu mori meu sangue ya cair na tua cabeça (If I had died my blood would have fallen on your head)"

I did not understand how she could say that to me; and then she told me that I knew of that women that; my father took me

85

to her house; of the same story I told her and she ignored me as always, but she told me that I did not tell her. I wanted to cry, and I remembered telling her straight after I arrived home and she was preparing me for my evening bath.

Speechless...

Luciana insisted that; she did toll her

I know that I told her, I remember everything and how I could not wait to get home just to tell mother, for some reason I felt like; it was very important that mother knew about that women and that night, especially because; firstly; I did not like that she was in private with my father behind my mother's back, and I doubted that she was somebody that mother knew.

Secondly; I just did not like her, and thirdly she looked completely ugly to me.

The day mother told me what was in her mind; I felt like I did not have a mother, I felt like; I meant nothing to her and that she personally had something against me. I wanted for GOD to come down and vindicate me because; I was wrongly accused by the only person I wanted to feel secure with; and it felt like I would always get some sort of emotional, and psychological torture from her 'I did not ask to be born'; Is what I used to tell myself, and I began getting tired of caring if she cared about me or not. It did not matter to me anymore. I used to look up to the sky whenever I was out

My silent cry to GOD 'GOD I'm lonely...'; that was the only thing that went through my mind after, I could not utter anything else. It was painful.

I always told mother everything whether it was good or bad, whether she would tell me off, reject me even more or accept me, and I never held any thoughts against her or anyone else; I was a kid. I took it and I looked to GOD to consol me and heal my wounds, as they were deep and wide holes.

Lucianna was then nine years old, and despite everything she always said that;; her mother was the most beautiful and kindest women she ever met, and her joy was that Lelo was safe far from Malto.

At last; she tells her mother about what Malto had been saying about her behind her back; Julianna was shocked "How can he be telling you this things, spitefully talking bad about me to youuu...! And you're a child! If he has problems with me he needs to address them to me, and not go you the child to insult me your mother"; Julianna sounded surprised, and disappointed. Most; of all she felt that her husband was on a satanic agenda to destroy; her relationship with her daughter, and then destroy Lucianna in the process. Lucianna was terrified that Julianna might have wanted to tell Malto; but she was not going to hide it from her mother or, keep it inside of her, and suffocation was taking its toll on her. She told; her mother not to tell her father, and that he had threatened her if; she had told anyone especially her mother, but Julianna was already angry with him. Hot headed as; she was waiting for Malto to get home for her to confront him. "Eu vou falar com ele"; said Julianna, completely dismissing Lucianna's request not to bring her name up because; she was extremely scared and worried about what her father would have done to her; at knowing that she did not keep it as a secret and told her mother instead of any other person.

The evening; came around and after midnight of that day; it seemed like; Lucianna was going to be alone, and she was going to have a restful mind and, be able to put an effort to learn English through the paper works Lelo gave her. Apparently; it was supposed to be a surprise, and all of a sudden he came from their bedroom to the living room. He was looking chilled, and ready... As soon as Licianna saw him; his calm a chilled posture portrayed that; he was coming to fill her head with more gossip and negativity towards her mother, as Julianna probably had not yet told him to stop by; confronting him about his conduct of late.

He walked in and said "You okay Lucianna?"; and I replied "Sím papa estou bem (Yes father I am fine)"; and straight from that moment I felt my heart trembling and sinking, about to explode with fear at the same time; while he pulled a chair to the side of the table, to sit exactly opposite me. I was nervous because; he was going to bring it up that part that; I became the listener to his immature, insensitive complains, and insulting back chatting he always did behind my mother's back. Once again he talked bad behind mother's back to me, and I felt regret of being there at that moment; as it was very inappropriate for me, and I did not want to hear it again. I felt like; he did not want me to be happy or, at peace with mother after rejoining her, I had missed her when I was in the foyer too, and I still wanted to try to be close to her and get along with her; at least after grown up if it was not going to happen when I was a kid. Even; if she did not think that it was a great need or, it had no importance to her; I wanted her to remember me, and know that I was around.

The next day I woke up late, at twelve o'clock in the afternoon, and he was not at home, but mother was and I had told her that the same tipe of conversation took place again when; I was studying after midnight. That time she seemed a little bit calmer; and that was the day, that she told him in their bedroom, but he denied it all, I was playing in the second bedroom; our bedroom, and the door was open and we were all indoor.

He walks out of their hotel bedroom fuming, his face expressed deep anger and hatred from the heart, and his eyes were all red; fiery red; and as soon as he saw me he stared at me and confronted me as though, I was his enemy. Angrily; he looked at me and straight away started attacking verbally me "Vôçe, vôçe eu te dice ou pue? Eu te dice para ires falar na tua mãe ou que eu te dice? (You, what did I tell you? Did I tell you to tell your mother what I told you?)"; he spoke with a strong aim to intimidate me, and it worked, I was stuck I did not know how to respond "Não"; but I stuck to the truth I answered, and he looked even more angrier "Falaste porque? Quem te mandou falar? Issto era entre eu e vôçe (Why did you say it? Who mandated you to speak of it? That was between me and you)", "proscima vez vais ver ou que vou te fazer. Soa burra. (Next time you'll see what I will do to you. You dumb head.)"; he told me. Scared I was; as I knew I had no one that would protect me in case

Mother, would not protect me from him and what he did, just like when he attacked me, she walked passed to the kitchen, and she heard everything, but I also did not expect anything good or bad from her!

However, I was thinking to myself while all this was happening, how can a father be two face and conspire to cause problems as such; turning children against mother, and mother against her children. This became a continuous circle in our home, he looks for a lone time with one child to gossip and conspire against the other, forcefully making the child come to conflicts against the victim child to team up with him. And, when the victimised child finds out his hope was always to see separation amongst one another, while turning to him for mutual support and attention to his satisfaction, but he did not succeed.

This was a disgusting repeated pattern of behaviour from him, since then nothing changed, things only had gotten worst.

I became adapted to the environment and I was accommodated back into the family, with souvenirs of the foyer; the bad times became attribute' of the good times transforming everything; summing up to an overall good memories.

'How sick, and disturbing that is...!'; Lucianna felt released, but little she knew about what he would attempt to do in the years ahead as she grew up. The constant forced attempt to enter into the bathroom and the toilet when she was there bathing, or taking care of her necessity, following her to the bathroom, and bedroom after; bathing. It was; a very scary and terrifying; and when she was dressing up he also walking into her bedroom on purpose. Just as he sees her stepping out of the bathroom going to her bed room, and ass soon as she entered into her bedroom and closed the door behind her then would also go after her, she after scolded him and kicked him out and closed the door back in his face after he opened to enter her bedroom. He taunted her with personal questions about her ladies problems and issues; Lucianna found it all weird and creepy, and him being out of line. He even wanted to know when she shaved her pubic her, how, what she uses to shave... all uncomfortable things, but she also used to tell her mother, and Julianna always made sure to tell him of his inappropriateness, insane and, disrespect.

"Was; he just too much of a man whore that, he also decide to pursue his own daughter to have sexual and inappropriate behaviour and actions?"; "I was not a kid anymore when he was doing those things and tried to kiss me on my lips, drawing his face close to mine pushing for a kiss, and I turned my face to the opposite direction and try to get away, and he attempting over again when he was wearing nothing but a towel. I was seating on the sofa alone in the living room, on a school day, as I was at home recovery from TB meningitis. I told mother; she told me "You're his daughter is normal, he wanted to give you a kiss"; she did not understand, and I told her again in details, and this time around she said "How can he try this? That is not normal, oh no, no, no! Next time he tries anything like this; tell him off stand up for yourself, and tell me, don't accept this, what is this man thinking, and trying to do?"

"I was fourteen years of age, and I had just left the hospital to recover at home being down and weak, and he tried that... but before that; I already knew, that he felt like; he could do and have anything he wanted and the rest of us just had to accept

90

it. Well I was never going to let anything be done to me, that I understood the meaning of it and, did not agree. Something disgusting, and dirty."

All these happened many year before; GOD told Lucianna to open her eyes when she was sleeping on the floor with the rest of the people in the house her family; Malto had called for a fast of two weeks when his mother passed away "Esses dias vamos dormir no chão durante duas semanas porque: a minha mãe morreo, e também tamos de jejum durante essas duas semanas, e vamos rezar para Deus abrir as nossas portas y tudo que estamos a fazer (We will also be fasting during these two weeks, as we will be sleeping on the floor during these two week because: my mother died, this is our fast, and we will pray for God to open out doors in everything we are doing)"; said Malto however; Lucianna and her mother saw it to be abnormal because; in the African culture and as Christians and true children of GOD fasting observation during a funeral mourning time, is not to be done. As, much as Lucianna was not willing to sleep on the floor, she decided because of the funeral mourning time, but not for the fasting and prayer that Malto had declared.

Behold; GOD spoke to Lucianna in her sleep; He told her to wake up and, open her eyes, to see so; she did, and she saw him, Malto laying down on the floor pretending to sleep, he had put his arm over his head, toward Lucianna, and started moving his finger, "It looked like; he was using signs to make signs for something, and they did not look like, normal movements..."; and with his other hand "His fingers were also moving making sign, and I straight away understood that, he was communicating with spirits, I understood that; they were sects satanic communications" "I straight away yelled at him looking straight at him "Que isso huh? (What is this huh?)"; and he lifted his head looking to me and hid his hands, and looked down again. Inside of me

I started praying and rebuking it, when he woke us up at six o'clock in the morning to pray, he wanted to hold hands, and he saw me standing next to him, and immediately he resented holding hands especially mine. He looked scared that I would say something in front of the other about what I saw, but I did not, and instead I told mother in private."; GOD wanted me to see proves and I did.

The Different Influences II

At home; it was always beatings, blows, shouting 'can't do that, can't do this, can't smile, can't play, can't joke with one another'. I liked being outside.

Whilst we were out in front of the church Tami was the only supreme complainer, and she often started of by saying that; she had no money and that she was very hungry with exaggeration and huge emphasis in her vocal expression of hunger. And, out of a sudden we would see her walking out of KFC again, with her belly full, and with an attitude, as of someone who says 'I don't care about you or what you think, I was hungry, and my money is mine I'm not sharing my food'; after I saw that, I thought to myself why must I ask around for sponsors from the others just that I can buy food for me and my 'best friend'; she came by where I and the others were, and she began to be loud again like; she always was her usual loud self. I then went out to buy a packet of chilly flavoured roast banana plantain at the newsagent, pay point shop that is three doors away from the door of the church leaving her behind. When I got back from the shop, I opened up the packet that I had just bought, and I asked everyone around the place if they wanted some banana, as I was willing to share with everyone, especially those who hadn't had anything to eat yet. Though some of them were still hungry and hadn't eaten anything throughout the whole day like; me they said 'no it's okay Lucianna, you have it to eat'; but with Tami she was the first person to stretch out her arm and opened her hand to deeped it into my packet of chilly roasted bananas plantain snack, and off she got herself a handful of my bananas, and she did not even say thank you, nor she was and looked grateful, and not acknowledging that; what she had taken to eat without permission did not belong to her. I didn't like what she had done, but I also said nothing, however I instantly judged her in my mind, for her very selfish, undisciplined and full of herself behaviour, and how she often acted like. Tamy often used to argued with Mariah.

Mariah was five years older then Tamy and I, and she was shorter then us, her voice was much softer then ours but; one of a little girl, I found her to be a beautiful young women, and she was kinder then Tamy. I looked at her like a big sister. I respected her to a certain extend, as in the house of the Lord we are all equal in His sight, His children for those with close and serious relationship with Him, but overall souls; and she was older then me. On the other hand; Tamy used to curse at Mariah, scream and shout in her face telling her to shut up; I personally did not know of their relationship in the past prior to me joining that church, and nor did I care about their relationship, as I went to church solely for GOD, but forced to be at that church. But; they would go back and forth arguing, Tamy used to get viciously angry and heated up; she used to hit the doors and the walls in the middle of their arguments yelling at Mariah, and screaming to the rooftops of the church, whilst Mariah used to get very upset during and after the scene Tamy often pull off; at the level of disrespect from Tamy. Mariah often stormed off crying and running to the ladies toilet to cry in hiding away from everyone else, she always found embarrassing to be crying in front of everyone, but even so we always saw her crying. She went to the toilet to also, take some tissues_

"Excused me: no she needed roles of toilet tissue paper"; to wipe her tears, look in the mirror, fix her make up, and then come back out again to be in harmony with the other members of the youth group the mirror was the most important accessory in the ladies WC. No body; ever found within themselves to get involved, in their arguments and fights not even the youth pastor of the church; the pastors actually would walk pass them or stayed locked up in the pastoral office. Mariah and Tamy's arguments were always; very catastrophic, and incomprehensive; I too like Lelo never understood the reasons for their arguments. I had started to witness the hostility between the two of them, from within the first two weeks I had started to attend the church and taking part in the youth group services; they both had continued with their argument till Mariah had left the youth group, and the church all together, but over the years I also; saw Tamy saying "Sorry Mariah for earlier"; and they would start speaking again, but that was only when Mariah had food. Mariah never used to say sorry to Tamy I guess maybe because; she felt that she had no reason to apologise to her, however Tamy definitely felt a certain way about that; and that was to become the reason for another argument.

Mariah was the type of person who seemed not to have a backbone for strength and authority; her own younger siblings who were also in the youth group were disrespectful to her in the church, not always but; also in front of the youth group. Although; I think it is normal; because siblings do fight and argue just like me and Lelo did back then. But; maybe if they didn't have their arguments in front of us, Tamy would not have grown wings to disrespect Mariah the ways she used to; Mariah is someone who is older then Tamy; and their sister and at that time Tamy and I were still under age not even fourteen years old both of us were still very young.

As, well as her character, personality and her fashion style; Tamy was the perfect example closest to the street environment with, one of the fashion trends that I used to see around outside on the street by; her visual appearance of what; a hype chick was, and looked like back when I was a young teenager. Back then I didn't have a description for girls of her style that matched her personality, but I now describe them as that 'hype chic'; they were loud. Always in the hype, ready to shout at and jump up on somebody, intimidated others, rude, disrespectful, they were very street aware. They knew when two gang crews would link up to beef (fight). The fights were mainly between two gang groups of different areas within the same borough or different boroughs of London especially between schools. Loud, and rude; she portrayed herself as tough she was an attribution of a top chic (girl). Tamy always had a boy friend and acted much more older then her age I don't even recall seeing the look of innocence in her eyes, face, character and personality.

It; was said around that; she used to use those boys for their money and that is why; she often engaged with them in a boyfriend and girlfriend relationship. She did not only engage with them because; she felt like she wanted and needed a boyfriend, but having a boyfriend was her way to get attention in the youth social circle, that she was in, as well as, it was for safety, I imagined as, she was always attempting to get my brother involved in her street battles to defend her from other boys. Tamy only had sisters, and she "I wish my mum can have a boy this time"; she used to say. I was always annoyed every time she did that; especially if it was when I was enjoying spending time with just my brother and, she happened to be there, and not minding that she was interrupting two sibling bonding time, by bring her troubles for my brother to handle. I used to think that she fancied Lelo sometimes...

Boys; it was also her way to financially conquer what she wanted that money could buy and she could not attain it from receiving her monthly allowance from her parents; alike many young people who don't receive a penny from their parents to live on. As; she often exclaimed, "My new boyfriend is really rich!"; in a low key as if it was a secret that she had a boyfriend; while everybody knew she always had a boyfriend. But it was a secret.

A secret kept from Temirah her big sister. Tamy longed to fit in the crowed and desperate for attention. She would flaunt her body in front of boys and guys that were much older then us by shaking her bum when she walked down the Croydon high street, school, to and from church, while she wore her cramped tops, loose flirty, waffle jersey, or pleated knee length skirts that equivocated sexual attention to her due to the way she moved her body. Her skirts used to draw out the shape and form of her buttocks and the steep trembling of her buttocks as she walked across from place to place in everyone's face. She used to wear a lot of stretch fabric clothing; especially for her skirts and jeans.

The boys used to comment on her big ass as so it appeared to be, they liked it and; she liked that too, but there were times that; when they commented on her body, but instead they judged her, and they did not like her, however she always missed those signed. In her head she believed that; every boy and man that had set eyes on her liked; her and what they saw. I wanted to help her

She was quite a numbskull in many things, almost everything, everything. She, preached to others girls who wore the same type of clothes as her to stop wearing it, and not to be happy if a boy liked it because; all he wanted was to use the girl. "Mmmmmm"; and yet she did not understand that all those boys wanted to use her too before spreading her phone number; giving it to every guy who asked for it.

How Tamy life is now is the result of her conducts throughout her growing up, she did not pay attention to her development, she did not pay attention to the moving course of her life. And it's sad. They used to look and stair at hair buttocks when she walked past them, and she would always look back to them, and flirt with the boys and guys with her laugh, body language movements and the battering of her eyes lashes. In the end before her departure from them, she always gave them her mobile number.

Tamy had never ceased an opportunity to have a boyfriend, she didn't care about what people thought, or said about her and 'poor mother of hers'; I always though, as Tamy never listened to her mother, and found her sisters to be unbearable. She often came across as an opportunist and attention seeker but; she was only a kid who refused good advices and disregarded positive influences, therefore she was bound to make many and huge mistakes from our young age; this had started from when she was under the age of eleven. Most of the times I was very embarrassed of her and I wished not to be associated to her in any type of way, just as she was of me for not being as the other girls of the street; the hype chicks, always in the hype and; dressing age inappropriate etc. especially during the last stages of our friendship. I had found no pleasure in the friendship we had, I was sad, when she saw me at church, bus station with my friends, and she used run toward us to kiss and hug my friends and blank me as if I was a ghost image of me; present but not seen. There were times Tamy didn't even look at me to acknowledge me not even as someone she acquainted through her church when she saw me; not to talk of being well educated and polite to compliment somebody she knew and claimed to be her best friend. When; she was hungry and had no food in her house and, so she ate with her best friend at my house. It was all too much for me to take it. 'What am I?'; I used to ask myself. I consoled her when she needed but in my adversities she rejoiced! And took no interest of how I was doing.

Lucianna did not know the wrong she did to her best friend. She just wanted them to be well as friends, she wanted to feel that she was cared, appreciated and loved by her best friend whom she loved and cared for too; and not used. Lucianna had her doubts about her former best friend Tamy; about her person when they first met especially; on the day she proclaimed herself to be Lucianna' best friend after following Lucianna to the church nearby pay point station shop that was only four doors away from the Brazilian founded church in London Road, and Lucianna bought her something to eat after the Sunday service when Tamy mourned numerous times saying "mmmm, I'm hungry", "I'm so hungry" and Lucianna felt sorry for Tamy; as she did not know how to turn away from that, without seeming to be rude, and stingy.

"When someone asks you for food to eat, and you have to give them, share the little you have with others; help others" I grew up around strong humanitarian values. My mother always told me to love others, share with others, and help others.

'At twenty two years of age after meeting many people, different types of people from different social culture; I have come to see and understand that people who want your help only want to take advantage of you. They want your help but they don't need your help'; and sometimes those who help; only help to take advantage of the needy.

I was sixteen years of age when I locked it off 'clocked it off it sound as if that was a lesbian relationship; yak!'; not at all never was that the case although; she tried once; I was shocked and became very careful of her. Tamy was with her new found friend also from the same church where we both had met. They were both inseparable, they were always together while we officially were still best friends of one another "It was so weird and that; she never even said hi to me whenever she saw me, nor spoke with me; even if I tried; but yet apparently best friends we were, how was that possible?". If she cared about me as her friend, and our friendship somehow I happened to be the last person to know her secrets and the things she did in general whether it was good or bad. That; was the ongoing chain type of affiliation Tamy initiated for and in the friendship through the treatment she gave me; that took place before Riella came to the picture but; it had gotten worst after Riella came around with no words. But; again money seemed to be her drive; when Tamy and Riella became friends Tamy made herself to be a stranger to me like she also made me a stranger to her. I had lost any left over interest to continue as her friend, there was no communication between the two of us anymore, and I didn't want to be associated to her anymore. Tamy's low lifestyle, behaviour and the envious, jealous, slutty and flirtatious character including the overall treatment I received from her, made me see that she was not the type of friend I should have and value. It all led me to end a four years of best friend relationship that; was never a real friendship from her part of the friendship; in loyalty and reliability. She was not worth calling 'a friend' to me; I led a different type of life, and I was never lonely, I had three friends from school, and they were of better quality then Tamy; though we never met outside school, they were friends that I was not ashamed to bring home to meet my mother, except from one. How I regretted from that point on; to naively have had her as a best friend, how I regret not studying her person before even accepting to becoming her friend; my kindness was taken for granted and it was not the first time. I met a wrong person for me to walk with, but I Thank GOD.

Many people think that doing your friend wrong is only when 'you back stab, gossip, profane the secret agreement made for the two of you between the two of you, physically fighting, when your friend steals your boyfriend etc'. "How can you be friend with someone who does not uplift you, and only disregards you?"; I remember her well, and when I see some of my friends today, especially the ones I had met in my years at university I see Tamy, and I tell myself 'I know who and what this is. I know what she is playing at', sometimes you must take your time to get to know people before completely disowning them after committing yourself in the friendship if; it was not done before the friendship, and just like; I'm taking my time to know Nelsa, but I actually don't have to. I didn't find anything good about the street top girls lifestyle types of friendships.

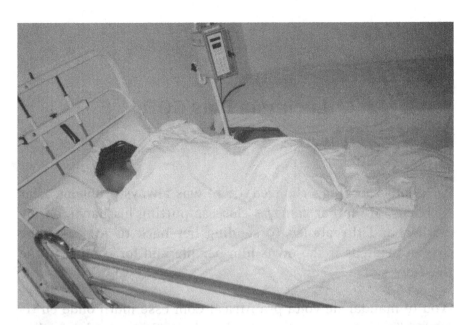

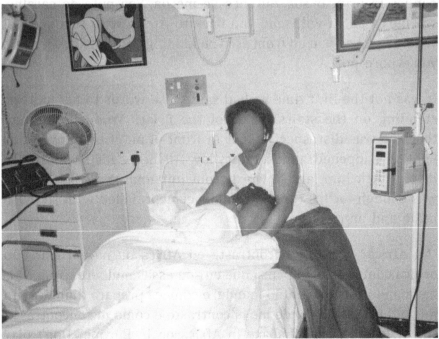

Lucianna Plus GOD

Back home nothing's changed, there was always problems after problems. My father came as close as putting his hands on my mother, and threatened to sending her back to Africa in the tone of pride as if she owns him her life and for coming to the UK. How sad.

"Vou te mandar de volta pra Africa! Com esse inutil onde eu tia panhei Ta brincar soa zairençe de merda, Soa puta do caralho, soa burra pa! (I will send you back to Africa with this useless! Where I picked you up from are you kidding you shitting Zairoise, you whore po!"

It was not the first time he had said these words to my mother; standing on the stairs inside of the Friars Wood house, and there he was disrespecting her in front of all of us in plain day light, it happened almost everyday. All he needed was to see Lelo, attack him, and a word from Julianna on Lelo's defence was enough for his threats commencement. Filled with so much pride and arrogance

"Na Africa? voçé me encontraste en Africa ou na europa? Não brinca com miguo, ta pensa que eu sou essas mulheres atoa. Vais me mandar devolta então manda, e começa prepara dinheiro pra mi voltar na Russa onde me encontraste e como me encontraste. (In Africa? Did you find me in Africa or, in Europe? Don't play with me, do you think I am one of these waist women. You will send me back, send me back then, and you better start preparing the money for me to go back to Russia where you met me up from and how you found me.)"

Mother's reply always remembered him that she was never a punk, desperate for him, or from a poor family and that if she was poor with him at that moment of life, it was because of him; and him on the contrary is the one who had an upgrade of class. Meanwhile; as they did not meet in Africa, and it was also mother who did everything for Malto to have a way out to escape. Arrogant. Blind. Selfish. Ungrateful and a irresponsible man. This man subjected his wife, his children, and us under his terror and he was proud of it his conduct I guess meant that 'he is the man'.

With the loud, and insulting arguments happening in at home; there were times that I was very surprised that non of our neighbours ever came to knock on our door to ask if everything was okay, or offered a hand in help to lighten the issues. I was even more surprised that the police had never knocked on our door; because a neighbour might had called the police; it was loud, the arguments, the yelling, the child beatings, and it felt very dark and lonely, and mother had no friends around. It was always my siblings and I there for mother. He used to threaten Lelo with the same thing. He would and still does things in purpose. Lelo would spend the night out sleeping at his friends house maybe also in the street; I pictured him in a street corner seated in the cold, sleeping leaning his head against a wall or a rubbish container many times. It breaks my heart, I feel sad to remember these things my emotions are immediately transported to the one of the past; when Lelo was still around living at home, before another disgraceful chapter of his life had began in December two thousand and seven, he was seventeen years old, and they did not document on that. Just seventeen years old.

Just at the brink of Christmas door the young lively boy, who was so eager to live and had dreams, but fell out of focus in search of acceptance, friendship and love the usual of what he did not have available in his home... on a dark winter Friday afternoon, Lucianna had arrived home before Lelo after college; there was no adult in the house it was only Uche, Benjamin and Essa at home, the lights were on, and as usual Lelo's friend used to used to pest him about the all the time to take him out to parties and be outside especially an older guy and his mother too who always went after Lelo for friendship. Julianna and Malto hated that; especially Malto he did not like that guy, but Lelo unlike; Lucianna had a very poor judgment on his choices of friendship "My brother trusted too much his friends, I guess it was due to the fact that they portrayed acceptance"; every single one of his friends have only proven to be hypocrites and two faced, and after the seventh of December some proved themselves to had be it out of the fact that; they were jealous of Lucianna's brother for a very long time. She describes their use of language in regards to him as he was taken away...

"It's a pity, that he valued friendship, and gave his loyalty to the wrong crowd, people and attraction; but he did not receive any love value from them; what they gave him was deception for his eyes filled in his heart "Don't be desperate for friends"; is what he used to tell me, and I thought he knew better; however he needed to feel that he lived that is why easily accepted but trusted so much in them. He probably thought that they were harmless to him; just like he was to them!"

Says Lucianna as, she speaks out her thoughts, whishing that he was stronger then what he was to resist the pleasurable invitations of his friend for parties, especially parties that were perhaps for people who were older then him, just as, some of his friends, and people he knew. Mother warned him about those friends, my dad also did, however he had a different agenda which; was of protection but of total destruction for Lelo. "Cuidado Lelo; these friends that you have are not good friends. Stop walking with him 'them'"; with a lot of care and attention to her son

Julianna would always everytime warn him and pull his ear about his friend. But; he needed friends, the only good friends that he had and whished they were still there within his reach so that; instead he would only walk with them, as he knew they were good children. They were three friend all from different continent of the earth, but they understood each other so well, they were very close to one another; I did not meet them, but Lelo and my mother spoke so much about them that at time I felt like I knew them very well. Malto on the other hand being him; he tried to separate the trio as; he always aimed at Lelo for even having good friends as those boys.

'If a friend wants you to help him or her but does not need your help; judge the situation first; don't be always just say yes; well it also depends on the type of friend that friend is to you. If a friend only wants you out with him or her to his or hers; and for the enjoyment of their interest that; only accommodates hers or his desires, wishes, and likeness; be on the fence; be careful; bring yourself back down, study that person and the type of friendship he or she holds for you. What is that person character like, behaviour, what are the words of their mouth like, how loyal and trustworthy are they? Remember that; just because you both share secrets of yours misbehaviours together, that is why they own you loyalty, reliability trust and believe and vice verse, it does not mean you must die with; or for that friend that friend might not be 'a ride to die for'.'

I guess that should be a sensible way of reasoning right?

That; guy that was with him on that day which; the police came to take him away, and Lucianna's father's words to Lelo in the early hours of that morning, was also there on the day that a prophesy fell from GOD to a pastor in the old church during a youth service while he was giving the testimony of his life. The young man was seen in the college he attended premises drunk with a knife on the day he had done what he had done before he had set her brother Lelo.

After college; Lucianna was at home when; her brother also was back after meeting up with his friends after college, and she remembers him, walking in the house and he seemed to be in the hurry, and excited like; he always was whenever he was invited to a party, going to eat out in Nando's with his friend's who knew how to eat, or out to promenades.

Lelo loved to eat, and food was one of his favourite things although; he did not eat a wholesome meal at home, seating at the dinner table with the family when breakfast if he could have it before going to school, lunch, and dinner; because he was never allowed to eat to his full satisfaction. Malto had a problem with it "Esse gajo, ca- é assím que se come seo caralho"; and then he would continue on saying "'You are greedy, why are you serving your self for the second time huh? Why are you finishing the food, are you the only person on this table? You bloody monkey. Put this food down!" '; He use to say that to Lelo and many more other things that many time made Lelo feel horrible 'it was as if Lelo did not have the right to eat, be pleased and feel comfortable'; on the table and any time Lelo took something to munch or, eat in the kitchen and Malto saw. "I could tell that; he was hungry"; says Lucianna.

But; mother also never said anything about that, her visual expression as that 'He is your father and he has to have the better portion and as much as he wants, I cooked for him'; without meaning by also; standing on her mother's duty mode. It always felt like he was the priority Malto; and the children came second, and it was the total contrary to what I saw, how I lived, and was taught in the foyer...

Living; there I guess showed me the proper way of leaving with others that and showed the responsibilities and consequences of life choices may bring to you someone's life that can change lives; I did not see in my family, and in many women. That was where I first heard of the saying "'Children first, then women, and then man" '; and I was intrigued "Wow! I like that..." I used to tell myself. Where I came from is man first, then your child although; children are priority but; depending on the standards and value a women may uphold for her child.

Malto served himself with the food on the table three to four time; creating a mountain of food in his plate, but he used to tell Lelo off at the table for wanting to have a second round of the delicious hot meal mother cooked. At home we only eat hot homemade meals, tat is how I picked up on cooking skills from an early age "I was okay, to help my mother in the in the kitchen"; I always viewed it as helping, even when; it didn't feel like it was to help. There was always plenty of food on the table ready, the table was always nicely, and luxuriously decorated and put together for every meal we took together in whole as a family, and when it was not used for meal. We never really lucked in food, and it was hard to see and understand why my father used to do and say these things to Lelo. Waking up in the middle of the night to sneak into the kitchen to eat food, if there was any leftover and, any food of the meal of the day left out of the freezer in the pan, and if there wasn't he used to just go back to his bed with packets of snacks to eat in his bedroom before going back to his sleep and wait for the next meal he was to have. And this went on; the last time he ate late was the early hours of the morning that; he was taken away by the police.

He looked confused, not knowing as to why the police was there at the door enquiring for him; there were three intense doorbell rings, and already Lucianna could hear Malto's voice from her parents' bedrooms "Assim vinherão para ou Lelo", "ELe é que entrou não? Saio de onde? vai abrir a porta"; Lucianna could tell that he was hoping that it was the police.

"Spera so, eu vou na policia presta queicha contra esse gajo, ele vai ver vou fazer de tudo para ele ir preso, seo bandido"; every time Lelo came home late from a party Malto used to say, that Lelo is a bandit and that he will go to the police station to press charges against him. He used to say that he will tell the police that Lelo is a thief, that he always steels at night as he is never at home, lying that he went to a party to cover his crimes. "I will tell them that he is a dangerous gang member he should be put in jail"; and every time he said does things he assuredly; expected an input from me usual he expected me to agree with him 'with laughter and excitement in my eyes and face as, I gave an evil input testimony against my brother'; he was excited and seemed to always have been looking forward to that day, the day which; his wishes were to come true! It was Malto who had opened the door to the police at four o'clock in the morning, it was dark and, very cold outside, my mother went down the stairs too, and became alerted too from when the doorbell rang three times, and that my brother had had just come from outside; a party I knew with that friend I guessed; and I was right. I could feel a certain electrical energy that smoothly arose from the tip of my finger to the rest of my body whilst fading away at the same time. I did not understand I felt that, or if it was in connection what was about to happen, but I knew that something bad was about to happen.

Deep down I saw a loud and harsh Malto busting out with a celebratory joy to his victory and accomplishment of what he wanted to have accomplished; all the previous years of our lives since before birth, before the seventh of December, I could also hear it in my head. "Ele vai ver so, acabo! Vais ir é devez esta vez não vais mas sair"; he told Lelo as the police handcuffed him. In me I thought 'what happened?'; Lelo got up from his bed as, my mother and I woke him up, and he walked down the stairs to the reception entrance door where they were all waiting to speak to him, but out of a sudden they said out the phrase "You are arrested", it was as if something ticked them in the head, and switched their mode. Lelo looking confused, calm and patient to find out too why was the police there and calling for him. They were; also on the radio communicating other polices, I think that were in the place of the scene, but at the time I could not understand. I thought it was a joke 'hopefully now you will stop being a friend with those boys'; I told myself in my mind 'Ignore dad and do not be with those street kids thugs, they are not helping you, and are always accepting them'.

It was a surreal moment, after Lelo got downstairs and was put on handcuffs, police forces stormed upstairs to his bedroom, and began a search, my mother were confused my mother especially; as the police force went into her house stormed into the bedroom of her three sons while two toddlers aged four and three were in bed sleeping "What are you looking for?"; and there was no word from any police man present, their posture and language strongly indicating that they knew not exactly as to what, and why they were searching his bedroom and carelessly minding that there were toddlers sleeping

"My two sons, there are children are in bed sleeping, in that room, can you please wait I'd like them to be removed first from their bedroom if you are going to be searching the room"; but it fell to no avail, I automatically went to their room and I carried Uche out of their bedroom, and Benjamin just woke up on his own, as the house was in movement and there were louder and unknown voices of the police that he had never heard. He was a kid, and worriedly he awoke form his sleep. When I went back into Lelo's room the police were already in the upper part of the house and in his room. Wanting; to see where to start with their search I found Benjamin seated on his bed, with his eyes about to get watery; whilst looking confused waiting to see if somebody he knew was going to walk into the door of his bedroom to explain to him what was happening or, maybe take him from there. So; I took him in my arms to my bedroom where I had left Uche, and I had put each to sleep on my single top bank bed. Beneath my bed Essa's bed, she was sleeping, but woke up briefly went out of our bedroom and also saw the police and, watch everything that had happened. "What has he done, and why are you here to take him"; and still there was no explanations, no word, nothing. By; then Malto was back in bed sleeping as if nothing was happening first; he cursed in front of the police, then he stood there to take pleasure in seeing what was happening to his son, because of false accusations and the words of his mouth and; then he left the dogs to have the remaining portion of what was left of his son; and leaving his wife to bare all. While; she was asking the police about what he had done, and where and which; police station they were taking him to 'the man of the house, the head of the family, the only person that GOD should use and speak to in the family for the family; he went to bed to sleep'; went back to bed sleeping till two in the afternoon; like a pregnant women who's days was filled with laziness, and tiredness. The next day mother received a call from an officer; who stated that we had to evacuate the house because; a team of experts as well as the police were going to come to our house for an in depth search, and so nobody was to be there, an that they also had to have a copy of the keys, but they would be working through all night. My father being how he was and secretly still is, was so quick and excited to agree, he felt important, just because, we had to sleep in a hotel and we were going to eat hotel food.

"You will not find anything in that house, my son is innocent"; my mother told the man on the phone after he drove us to the hotel and while he drove us to the hotel. The police refused to tell the mother of the seventeen years old boy about, what the charges against her son were, or what was going on altogether including the defendant; the seventeen years old himself.

The police was given access to the house and to work, before we left the home it was in good states, there was electricity, gas... everything was in place. However; when we returned home it was a different story that we found ourselves in, a story that could had ended the life of Uche, Benjamin, Essa, me, and mother Malto was looking for a parking space to park his car.

The house was dark, with curtains open and dirty, we switch on the light but, there was not light, so mother went to check the electricity and gas metre outside of the house, it read zero pounds for the electricity, and one or two pounds for the gas. Inside the house it was smelling, the house had a very strong scent that I had lost and left wondering about it's sense because of its intensity... I walked into the house with my younger siblings first; we all noticed the smell.

"Ta cheirar ouque?" Uche asked Julianna when she entered into the house, "ta cheirar! Essi cheiro é de que?"; Benjamin asked as soon as he entered into the house when I had entered "mama essi cheiro é de que?" he asked his mother when she came in. "Esse cherio é de gas, sím.. isso é gas, eles fizeram ou que aqui?"; she replied Benjamin whilst rushing to the kitchen, disappointed, and not happy at what the police had done, leaving no electricity, and the gas in the kitchen open. We left the doors and windows of the house open, and mother thanks GOD for what did not happen on that day that could have happened within second of setting the our feet back into the house that day. After; switching on the lights, and they did not turn on, because the police had used up all of our electricity including the emergency electricity from our metre, and did not bother to buy to return what they had used. Mother's instinct when she heard us from outside saying; that the lights in the house were not turning on was that I had to use the alternative for he while she; was checking our metres. "Lucianna acende a vela!"; she screamed from outside with the house front door open, I could not see anything, the house was dark, so I told Benjamin, Uche and Essa not to move an inch and not to touch anything. Up the stairs I walked fast, but attentive and cautious of the hazards exposed in the house at that moment and day although; every day became a threat soon after. I opened the white cupboard in the wall on top of the stairs, I put my hand through and, fiddled till it had caught a object that felt like; I touched or grabbed the candle with my hand. I was fast with it; I found three candles faster then

I thought I would, so I went back downstairs with all three candles, as the whole house was dark I figured that; we could use lightning in different areas of the house, however when I got down the stairs mother was already inside, worried about the gas smell, she went to the kitchen and checked the cooker and found every burner was left on. 'How irresponsible of them'; I knew that that officer who did this did not care about the lives he was endangering by doing what he did.

Alike; mother and I told him; he was not going to find anything of crime in that house, because "My son is innocent", "my brother is innocent. The simple fact that he found hard to defend himself with words in the law just as, he was not aware of anything that had happened that resulted to his arrest also; indicated his innocence, and to make it worst; there were many evidences that were kept hidden from the court judgement. We prayed, and prayed day and nigh on my way to college I also prayed and read my bible for him, I believed that GOD was going to come through, I encouraged Lelo to be strong, and I wrote to him everyday is not every three days. Praying for my brother became the only reason I wanted to pray for; leave myself aside, I made a vow with GOD in confidence, I looked up to Him more than I did for myself when I was in the Foyer.

On a Monday afternoon; Julianna and Lucianna went to work we arrived at work just after the late afternoon new had finished, and as soon as the security man saw Julianna, he sympathised with her, and said "Your son was in the news today, they said a lot of things, a lot of negative, the called him name"; Mr. Keith usually updated Julianna what was going on with what the media was saying about Lelo and his case and how he was portrayed. Lucianna was thankful that her mother often missed watching the news in those days; there were slurs thrown at him, they have deformed his image and name, they called him all sort of name including branded him racist. Lucianna remembers the way the policeman who had come to their house and was in communication with Julianna in early stages of the tragedy in regards to the searches conducted by the police to have been a very rude dismissive white man; who came across as racist the entire time he was in contact with the family. At; that moment his racism was not a priority, although it had triggered Julianna and, her children "It was a pity, the way he treated us, leaving the cooker burners on, the gas running out, not minding about the consequences of what and how the deadly hazard he display was to do to the family"; says Lucianna. Lelo himself suffered maltreatment at the police station from that same man who left the gas running with the house unlocked after their search. And evil conspiracy it was; against the family... the wanted to kill us. Uche and slowly started to get bullied and quickly became a target of child isolation by the other kids, the other family started to spread lies at the primary school Benjamin, Uche and Essa attended. They painted my brother's face with a lie, which the press then took advantage to fabricate many other lies. Stealing; his innocence trading it for their nephew, cousin subconsciously, Lelo did not know of their plot... Apparently; he had no parents. He lived as a pagan and a street kid without any parental or, guardian authority over him 'No wonder why'; he would call Lelo at every and any hour of the night to chat, and show up at our house to ask, borrow, or pick up Lelo's clothes for him to wear not Lelo when Lelo was not at home. Mother disliked it, I never gave anything unless Lelo overly begged to "Allow it, don't be a bad man"; this is what he used tell me. He lived in two houses, one which; belonged to his uncle, that was never according to him in the house, and that whenever he lived there he used be alone in the house. He said that the bills were left to him or whoever to pay, that boy used to Lelo to always help him to pay the rent of the house, making him feel uncomfortable that his friend was about to be homeless, because his uncle the owner of the house never paid rent and hardly lived in the, and his aunty disliked him, and that he had nobody to help because his parents are; supposedly dead. Once; the boy got arrested he had permanently moved out from his house to Scotland, and his aunty desperately wanting to talk to my mother in our house; my mother became even more alerted of that family, she never trusted them, never wanted her son to be friends with that boy but Lelo was trapped in feeling sorry for that boy; neither did mother or I ever felt sorry that boy. I on the other hand could care less about his story, I used to feel that; he either lied about it, or uses to manipulate people by the way he used to come to our house ringing our doorbell everyday to call my brother out, at times, and how easier is it to manipulate a child innocent, that thinks that; you are a friend of his or hers just because you are a good friend to him or her?

Nevertheless; that did not stop mother from doing what she could to protect Lelo, and every time that she and that boy met by walking past each other, or standing at the same location when I gain he would tail Lelo around to take him out mainly away from home and our family. She always; asked him and even escorted him many times before to his house to find out where he truly lives, and to also have words with his aunty letting; her know that she wanted her nephew far from Lelo, and away from our door steps... it was very hypocritical that boy and his family knew where our house and address; they knew where our house was at, but not one person that matters in Lelos' life, and had direct responsibility on Lelo as, his sister, mother or father knew anything about them. They would get half way to that boy's house and he would tell my mother that he forgot where about his aunty or; uncle's house is 'the place he lives, and should be going back to at the end the end or before the day ends'; my mother used to feel played as if she was his friend, or another kid from his block, or wherever he came from and disrespect at the level of serpent and of a snake. "That boy is a stupid kid, and I don't want him around my son"; my mother used to say, even when she did not vocally made a sound with her mouth at times, I could hear her thoughts when her eyes caught her and I was with her. He even had our house telephone number that he used to call to speak to Lelo, but I don't think Lelo ever had that boy's house telephone number.

Julianna had had enough, she wanted to have words with his auntie, or whoever was in charge and bringing that boy up; he had no manners, never said good morning, good afternoon, goo evening or, goodnight julianna once asked him "Are you just uneducated or is it manner that you lack in? Do you not know how to greet an adult, or people in general especially standing in front of your friend's mother, and in front of my house door what do you want here?"; and he was quiet staring at Julianna's face with his trousers down to his knees and a long, big baggy short sleeve t-shirt that looked like he was wearing Madea man version cloths. His long chin and arms abnormally long that did not even match his whole humanly body proportion, Lucianna's uncle used to call him monkey "Here, There is the monkey"; because of the supper long lengths his arms, it was not to be mean, but it was the way he portrayed himself with his character, personality and appearance.

He told lies, many lies on what happened on the seventh of December he twisted the truth to take Lelo down with him, or instead of him or the criminal. However; more and, greater then Lucianna's and Julianna's prayers, and everybody who prayed for Lelo, is His purposes, GOD's purposes.

The devil is a liar; he hangs around your life waiting to devour you; he is not too far from you. Check your family, some relatives, and your friends well, don't just believe in the obvious 'that is life, he or she loves me because... And we walk over our problems'; the obvious is what is in front of your sight. There is so much more to a human being then what is primarily seen which; is the flesh, the colour of the skin, the thickness of the skin, the external beauty, and the forefront character. Though we will not all win Oscars but we can all do a little acting. We all have a spirit, soul and heart; our skin houses them. What are your values and what values does your friend add to your life?

'Show me who you walk with, and I will tell you who you are'

I have heard that saying so many times, especially when I was just a pre-teenager; I guess mother felt the excruciating need to teach me about choosing my friends and the people to associate myself with right. But; I am also very lucky to turn out to be a strong-minded person. I knew from a young age who I am, had already had set goals for myself. In 2005 I was told that I would never be the same again, and that the things I used to do and was specialised in; I would never be able to do them again. I was told that I would not be like any other child of my age. I would never be normal again if; I survived.

However; at the turn out of things I guess; maybe GOD was giving my mother and I a chance and new beginning to our relationship. I was too alone prior to that. If I didn't turn to her she would not turn to me to give me the love, but she was also my only support system and my biggest and harshest critic. The words of her mouth, and how they were said many times deep down I asked myself, if that was love from my mother?

It was hard to accommodate the harshness all the time; but I kept quiet. Like a child who when she gets put in the naughty corner without fault; forgot of the harsh punishment after been taken out of the naughty corner; so did I.

When I tell people about what has happened to me; they don't believe it; especially friends who were not there at the time I had gone through what I went trough and they try to minimise the favour and grace of GOD that was manifested in my life. Why are you arguing strangers? You were not there, you saw nothing and you probably hadn't seen it because you don't believe that GOD still does miracles and is alive. Well I say shame on them, because they will never see GOD'S greatness in their lives; like I saw it in my life. My first step was my believing; even in my state I believed that I was going to be fine and, walk again; doing the things I love to do. And I saw it. Who saw me in two thousand and five is a witness. A living testimony I am. He is too great, and wonderful to me.

Lucianna doesn't recall clearly how it happened, but on her own account; it was a Friday morning after many years of complaints about feeling unwell with strong and constant headache, and rushes appearing on the surface of her skin all over her body and her face was filled with them. Light had become irritating for her skin too, and every day she had a different spot on her face, but it was believed by her doctors that it was due to her puberty. They turned a blind eye on every symptom and subscribed her Paracetamol, for the headache and different types of gels on different occasions for the spots and the blackheads (rushes) she had on her face, but nothing helped Lucianna, and she was given nothing for the rest of her body.

She was getting worst every day, but nor one doctor ever thought of neither suggesting a blood test to find out what was happening with her. The frequent complaints of headaches were recurring over the years, for so many years as long as she remembers. Lucianna remembers once being in her country, in her Futungo home when she was eight or nine years of age on a Saturday morning around half past eleven in the morning. A; very sunny day it was; but it was also too early for the heat wave to strike on the city. It was a cool and fresh Saturday. It was a peaceful morning; and a day with no conflict between her and her brother, as they had silent arguments in Lucianna's mind everyday; and were troubled for their disagreements everyday too. Except from, Lucianna was not at peace with herself physically; her head was banging very hard that she could not contend herself, she was at home with her brothers and sister and; they were in the house with their nanny. Juliana had gone out to a town near to the old town the family lived in before moving to Futungo to visit Lucianna's auntie who is Juliana's younger sister.

Lucianna felt as if she was being punished for an unknown reason, that Saturday along with every Saturdays during her growing up years was her biggest fear. Her heart bit was racing fast; she felt as if her blood was boiling, she was weak. She could not contend herself. She couldn't. Her head was too heavy for her and weakening her body, sucking up her energy, she trembled internally and could not say what she was feeling. She could not speak. She had told her mother once she got back form her visit that; she had a strong headache, and Juliana gave Lucianna a half tablet of paracetamol as; she felt Lucianna was too young to start taking full tablets of painkiller.

Lucianna believes that somewhere someone had spoken and done something for her life against her life progress, success and existence with the aim that; her end would be soon on a Saturday. But; GOD has magnificently and greatly confused all her enemies from birth, and who still fight against her to destroy her life.

She sat and hardly enjoyed herself playing on the floor, as the floor was the only place she felt better on though; it had not made any changes to how she felt during that excruciating headache. The later the day was the worst the headache had gotten. She rolled around the veranda floor in pain mourning her pain with no tears flowing from her eyes; and trying to have fun at the same time as she rolled around the veranda floor. The pain was too strong for her to cry out and loud. She remained strong, and fought to see herself through that Saturday like; she fought on many other Saturdays.

Many people say 'when you have headache you need to sleep, a rest will help it to go down'; but Lucianna could never sleep, whenever she had those headaches. Her form of resting was, sitting and rolling on the open-air, fresh and cemented veranda floor of her house while; her mother was cooking in the kitchen with the door wide open keeping an eye on Lucianna and her siblings also; and left Lucianna to rest. Lucianna used to only stay on the floor for the whole day till evening. At early evening she got up from the floor; took her bath, hardly had her dinner, watched television 'novellas Brazilleira'; and at last she falls asleep on the sofa, and her dad then carries her to her bed when he got home and found her asleep on the living room sofa. Lucianna used to wake up in the morning on her bed and wonder how she got there, she only remembered sleeping in the living room sofa, but she also used to think 'father carried me last night and put me to sleep in my bed!'; Lucianna used to like that her father used to carry her from the sofa to her bed every after work for; as long as she was sleeping on the sofa.

Every night Lucianna went by through to the next morning, she woke up with blooded nose. Her nasal holes blocked inside and out; and her nose was covered with dried blood, she never used to understand what used to happen to her during the night when she slept. None; of the adult around her could explain nor; had an answer as to what was happening to Lucianna at night when she had put her head to rest on her pillow, and covered with under her duvet cover.

Along the journey in her days of headache, Lucianna developed many other symptoms, and al were ignored by her doctors or better; GPs doctors, she went into her appointments countless time; she expresses and; complained about all the symptoms she sow developed in and on her body and she had no idea why she got them, the doctors prescribed nothing but Paracetamol. Paracetamol prescription has killed many people, and doctors have turned blind eyes onto the real cause of illness and disease and it's appropriate cure from the selective prescribed medicine for cure.

On that Friday morning, Lucianna had gotten unconsciously brainless, weak, emotionless, but all she could do was complain that she was feeling headache "Mama cabeça ta mi duer comforça" and Juliana interpreted to the doctor anything Luccianna had said; it was all about her health and well being now. In her very strong French mixed with African accent Juliana translated but this time around Lucianna laughed not at her mother but; tried to correct her pronunciation of English the words "mãmãn! Não é assím que se fala. É ar não hrrhhhh. Fala denovo", while she laughed she used to correct her mother's pronunciation.

That; in itself told Juliana that the case of her daughter was critical, the sudden change in what she was accustomed to getting from Lucianna her daughter's half misbehaving and half joke treatments towards her. Luciana's silence after her mother's interpretation to the doctor of what she had said made Juliana feel not completely with her daughter. Her soul was already missing Lucianna. And she was highly alerted. 'Something is wrong with my daughter'; she told herself, as she slowly walked into her despair for her daughter back and well. Lucianna's cure depended on the doctors now, and always did. Nothing was concluded at the medical general practice on that same Friday that; could have saved Lucianna's life from the death threat of her illness; because they were negligent. No; early diagnoses, blood testes, close attention to details of health and physical changes and complaints of Lucianna; would had have prevented that day from happening. Typical government health service system. It was too late for medical prevention.

At the hospital Lucianna and Juliana's only hope and help was GOD. Lucianna had under gone a series of blood tests, and scans and this age and time she does not remember their names. One of the sides effect the illness and disease had left Lucianna with, is called forgetting which; now affected her neurological system. Lucianna describes her hospitalisation journey as exhausting, tiring, abnormal, deep, 'mystique' so as her mother always said since Lucianna fell ill and hospitalised. How; everything happened "I agree with her", says Lucianna.

I was transported form room to room to have different tests done, as I was taken from room to room and from one department to department; I was loosing myself; I had no sense of judgment and self control; my body had lost total balance, and I could not be held still. My body trebled and the trembling went on for the 24 hours whether I was awake or asleep my body trembled; with all my senses lost, I could not tell if; I was feeling cold or if it was just the effects of my weak health state. I was getting weak and weaker by the second and as each second past I was also; loosing bits of information about my identity. I suffered very high memory lose; were by the time I had made a significant progress in my hospital bed, I did not remember anything. I had stayed at Mayday for a day or two if not then between hours.

But; Lucianna has no clear memory of the time frame of the course of event.

I was there for a very short period of time but long enough to call attention from the many different hospital members of stuff including the people that were not doctors or nurse to my case. My; health state had instantly become a case study to find what was going on with me; my health. Especially for the doctors. It took extreme hard work, and very close attention to details from the doctors, nurses and lab specialists and whoever else took part in the process to uncover what was wrong, and going on with me. While on my stay at Mayday I had become numb, paralysed and senseless and a fluid from my spine had been taken from my spine for the necessity to discover what was wrong with my health with significant life risk which ran high each second that passed me by; when I was laying down in my hospital bed. Indeed; the results were out of the doctors... The human scientific knowledge for cure. This test was done twice on me, the first time it was taken; the result showed absolutely nothing; my mother's heart busted out of her chest in shock, terror, but contending patience in her that; things were going to get better. She knew not how, but she knew they would. 'When you trust in the living GOD, with your whole heart and life, and when you put him first, He will reveal Himself in your life and of your significant ones; to be who He said he is; '"the Beginning and the End the Alpha and Omega"'.

Mother did not trust that; the condition was going to get better, doctors, husband who was useless in this case for; even simple support just like; in many other cases as, mother had stood up alone and recharged herself with the celestial army of GOD whilst father start to play 'pretend I care and worried; after days the occurring situation'. Prayer group, and pastors were not seen in my ward; except once or twice a pastor came in to the hospital to pray for me. Relatives, the doctors and the nurses were a good support especially the doctors. They are the people that GOD chose and anointed with the wisdom and knowledge to save lives on earth; whether; they are able to perform their duties and task or not. In my case, they were there medically, but mother also saw that; they cared; as the took interest in my case and to want to see me well; they also started to believe in GOD for a miracle for me... Even; when did not have to see me in a particular day; they still came to my room to check on me and speak to my mother.

After the fail of the first test, before the fluid was taken from my back for a second time mother anointed me with the anointing oil and; she prayed to GOD; she pleaded with GOD in her motherly cry out to GOD and. She reminded GOD of the times that; she knew of the things I had done to contribute to the work of GOD in church and outside the church. My mother reminded Him of the every Saturday early morning that I went to church to clean the house of GOD after; doing my part of the chores at home. She reminded Him of the offerings I had presented to Him even when I had nothing for myself as; I and my siblings never received anything from my father's own money what; we especially me and Lelo used to get was the government monthly allowance. Our monthly; child benefit allowance. Even for us to receive that; it was so hard for us to receive that from Malto because; he felt entitled of that money. Whenever; we received any of our child benefit money it was five to ten pounds a months meanwhile; we were entitled to forty pounds per month. How pathetic; we were dependent of that money to buy clothes, shoes, for me as a to pay the hair dresses to do my hair. Lelo's foot used to grow every month, and he always needed new shoes and trainers for his size however; he never asked for money; he knew that he was not going to receive his forty pounds child benefit allowance from dad; instead he was going to get insults, and so he would turn to mum for everything that concerned him.

I used to spend that money in weekly bus pass to go to school, buy a top if I could afford it with the money I had left at the end of the month, and I also it buy something to eat whilst out when I was not at home for the day. Usually; I only used to buy one packet of crisps, or a lolly pop but I didn't buy these every time that I was out as 'I had to save some money for tomorrow'; for myself. It took extreme money management. And, whenever I had ran out of money and I asked my dad for more he just never wanted to give and never gave anything. "That is your problem"; he often told my mum, if there was anything missing at home and she asked him for money to buy what was missing for food etc. It; could have been as little as a bag of rice, or a tin of chopped tomatoes to prepare and make a cooked meal for the day for the family. When; Lelo needed money to buy his new school shoes, buy his pants or socks, sometimes the money Lelo used to ask for was to help him buy a bottle of water to drink on his break at his football training session and to pay for his bus fair to go to his football training luckily; his coach often offered to pay for his bus fair to make things light on my mother's side.

Lucianna personally never got a straight forward 'NO' answer.

My father used make me believe that he would give me and provide what I needed and asked for but; he never accomplished his word, from the age of twelve I saw the words of his mouth not to be trust worth and in vain. I had started to doubt him, and his words, never believing in his promises; because they were and are nothing to him. But; I understand it 'he does not have to fulfil anything he does not want to. But; why does he makes promises?' "I now know better then to trust you... through so many things and faces you have shown and continue to show us and everyone else. It is unfortunate; that those who don't know you think that they know your father."

And till this day; my dad is similarly the same as how he was fifteen years ago, and if anything has changed; he has only gotten worst by every breath he takes. He is still that same greedy and selfish man, father, and husband; that man who is guilty but hide behind his wife's skirt, and expects her to clean up his dirt and tide his mess and that man who only cares about himself.

In my time of illness, near death, near to perdition, mother bowed down her knees to GOD without hesitation in her strong will and lifted her head and hands to GOD for me, for His grace and favour on me.

What a beautiful mother I have! She reminded Him of the midnight hours prayers I often made as a sacrifice and appreciation for the fresh breath air for the living He gave me, and the eager to know Him more and more; while many people and those of same age as me had given them selves to the world at; the influences of the devil. I did not keep Jesus away He was the best I knew and still do. I was mocked, I was called a freak, boring, looser, young people of the world wanted to make me feel fear, and girls hated me they looked at me up and down. I also; had false friends who wanted to use me for my kindness, but I told GOD I'm stuck with you, and I immensely feared Him with my life. I knew and still know no other way of true living but through Jesus Christ of Nazareth what; I saw through Him has made me to not forget Him. His is pure and extraordinary. I never wanted to disappoint Him. Oh no! I found no interest in the lifestyle many young people were following I saw it as a waist of lifetime grace. Lucianna realises how light headed she gave her mother during her years of growing up, during the good and the bad times. She was a good child who knew and wanted to learn to fear GOD.

Hours after my mother had anointed me with oil I was taken through the second round of CSF collection, and this time around the hidden illness showed its face of shame.

The test result gave a clear answer to what the illness and internal problem was, and the physical distortion. However; spiritually there was another battle that; only Jesus Christ prevailed once again of course, just like always when He is called upon and believed in, He grants victory to the people. Regardless of; ones background, culture, birth religion, or family status. We all matter to Jesus and we are all the same. When GOD looks at us; He does not see, our bodies, the designer clothes, our heights, body mass, or the colour of our eyes and skin; He sees souls. That is all; souls.

The doctors discovered Lucianna's illness. From the moment that the result had come out, Lucianna was confirmed to be a TB Meningitis positive hospital patient in the intensive care unit. My health was only deteriorating with the chances of survival; given the fact that she'd gotten worst by the seconds, and she had to be transferred to St Georges because Mayday can not treat TB meningitis.

At St Georges still unstable very weak and unconscious. Lucianna's mother prayed all the time and sang all day long every time she sang; something moved in Lucianna that led her to sing along songs of praises and worship to GOD with her mother. Juliana describes Lucianna to be happy and at ease when she sang. "It was a miracle happening before my very eyes. Ou que DEUS fez para ti Lucianna?" (What GOD has done for you Lucianna?) Mesmerised says Juliana, and many times there were other girls in the youth group, especially one girl who always told me the same; with another mesmerised mind sound of her voice. Then she made a loud clicking sound of contemplation of what GOD had done using her tongue in her mouth "Ntln." Juliana was marvelled. When; she saw and heard Lucianna sing along with her in her moment of unconsciousness without the knowledge of speech, unable to speak, move and thoughtless, but the only thing she could do was sing praises to GOD "hallelujah!"; Juliana was happy, though the road was long; and she did not know what the end was going to be like. But; it gave her strength to not give up. She held on to her faith, she held on to GOD and she grabbed on Jesus' mantle for her daughter.

Juliana had moved to live at the Hospital, to take close care and give attention to her daughter and closely watch the development of Lucianna's state. Juliana took to the hospital in a little suite case her belongings and few of Lucianna's things; pyjamas, under wears, socks, comb, teeth brush and body lotion.

Lelo went to visit Lucianna whenever he could and also; called her most of the times during her stay in hospital.

Very tired, and feeling hungry but I could not swallow food except from porridge and I had to be fed by my mother if I were to eat or, drink water. However; I had not eaten for the first few days if not one week after being transferred to St. George. I was weak unconscious and motionless; mum did everything for me from; the day I fell down ill and I was taken to the hospital. Malto told my mother not to move to the hospital to stay with me but; we know why; after all, all he ever did of himself was sign up to the jobcentre for benefit, and take English classes over and over as if he knew not how to speak English, write or read. Though; he had a very strong accent but; who does not? Born English speakers of different parts of the United Kingdom also have different accents. Some; are easy to be understood, and others are just not easy to understand one single word.

But that was Malto's excuse not to work. It was evident he did not want to work to support his family. When my mother was working on two jobs one that made her leave the house as early as; three o'clock in the morning, and another starting in the afternoon at half past five in the afternoon while; my father was in the house seated watching television, talking on the phone gossiping with other man of his party about other man, eating before and after beating Lelo. This was Malto's daily routine. And he did not want my mother to move to the hospital, because he was worried about the cooking of food at home.

I also remember once upon a time; my mother worked in four jobs a day with low wages pay rate from each job, to pay the bills at home, to buy food for the family, to supply her children's educational needs paying for trips if she could afford to pay for our school trips. But; one of her jobs never used to pay her; even after she decided to leave the agency, they still did not pay her wages of the period of time that; she had worked for them. Mother's money always fell short, and was not once; ever enough. If not; she used to tell us "'to go and ask dad'"; and there was; a wave of questions to face from my father and answer, as if he was not our father that he relented to provide and deliver to our needs but; an estrange investigator handling an interrogation to find out if the year group head teacher was ripping him of. As; though he had worked so hard for that money or the school requested millions of pounds from us to be able go to the single school trip. Forgetting that the money he used to pay anything for us was not his, but it was from the child benefit money income. For many years since the family eloped to the UK seeking political asylum my father did not work, actually since he escaped from my country even when; good jobs opportunity came his way he shattered it and chose to live off benefits.

My mother and father were eligible to Jobseeker's Allowance and; my father had declared for him and mother but; she never touched nor received any penny from it. My father used to collect it and stuff it in his pocket! His and hers. We used to wonder what he used to do with that money, what investment exactly he made for the family? With life being very low to the ground nothing made sense and nothing's changed only discoveries being made.

I remember once; when he was comparing my siblings and I to his nieces and nephews in Africa, he especially did the comparison on Lelo. He would start with;

"Voces não prestão para nada. Çues burros, cabrõens, ous meus sobrinnhos estão lá en Cabinda são maís espertos que vôçes, seus burros."

And; then he used to start telling Lelo "Tu es um burro, seu cabrão de merda! Eu vou te mandar de volta en Africa, Vais la para Cabinda e mando vir ou meu sobrinho aqui seu cabrão, pensas que eu preciso de ti?"

He spoke these words with an angry arrogant tone putting fear in us; he thought so. Showing absolute careless for his children including his daughter he made when he had a affair; cheating on my mother back in my country with a Rwandese women. She died shortly after giving birth, never mentioned as to how soon or later...

My dad's entire family and friends knew of this betrayal, and when my sweet mother took it upon herself to raise the child and bring her up as hers after finding out of my father's betrayal; my siblings and I still to this day are known to have no clue of his infidelity and man whore ways of Malto. It is a running train track with this man. The appearance of a family man is the perfect cover he has always used to hide the dirty truth about him.

How I wish he were exposed from his inner person and out! The dark spirited soul that he is. A man who claims that; the spirit that lives in him is the right spirit. The Holy Spirit of GOD; but yet change has not been identified to have taken over him. A total conversion in need, and his actions are showing that he does not and neither; will he ever change.

Her mother bought books, paid for the internet at home which; was forbidden to be running in the house; which, Malto once told Julianna to prostitute herself to pay for the internet at home for us; she bought our schools uniforms, school shoes, school bags, pencil cases, equipments, and any toys we had. When Lucianna was thirteen years old; she felt tired and worn from her family life. To ask her father for things she needed and never received them and mal receiving half of what she demanded through her needs. "I did not think or feel it was fair that I should chase the 'person who lived in the same house with me, my father for him to deal with his duties'; when I lucked, it did not matter to him." Malto made it to be not his business if any of his children were in need, including his wife Julianna. I remember once he took the whole household benefit income; all we had and depended on to live and sent to Cabinda his family, and said that it was for the business there, and that GOD was going to provide for us. He continually sat at home, and mother embarked for her many jobs a day twenty-four seven.

Lucinna was raged, angry and disappointed, as always, she has never met anyone who failed to disappoint her, letting her know that Jesus surely has never disappointed her and is the only one who has fully had her back, and teaching her to be patient. Being patient; for the good thing of life that owe to her following her hard work and placing GOD first and Jesus with her. With no food at home to eat; mother had to manage on her own as of a single mother.

Many times I asked her this question "why are you still with him?"

Leaving her lousy and lazy terrorist husband who to this day refuses to pay the bills at home, and help his wife with anything, including their children as Lucianna describes him to always have been at home, and pretends to always have been a man and father who takes good care of his immediate family to the public. Seating on the sofa, watching TV, and eating at home and to also find out at the end of the day that her husband had been abusing Lelo behind her back and intimidating the rest of them. A lady; at the primary school where Uche, Essa and Benjamin attended; was once very worried and, wondered what was going in their house after seeing Benjamin crying numerous times in school, and on his way to school and always looking sad with a long toddler face. One day she decide to ask little Benji, what was wrong, and Benji told her how Malto was with them at home especially with Lelo, and that he could not take the atmosphere and dynamic of terror Malto created at home. The; lady became worried, and felt increasingly; sorry for Benjamin she could not wait to meet Julianna to have a chat with her at the school "There is a lot that goes on, I am not surprised that my toddler is strongly affect; and everything he told you is true and there is worst going on daily"; Julianna sounded desperate, and willing to take any adequate help for her children first. After few conversations the lady gave her a parenting class card for Malto to consider... Julianna was happy of the help, and hopped that; Malto would somehow; feel a comprehensive and take parenting class to learn better ways to communicate at home and become a better father and husband, as she was willing to go too. However; Malto looked at it; and said I do not need this, it is not important for me. In those days of terror Lucianna used to wait for her mum to get home from her last job of the day in the late evenings before she had to leave for work again in the midnight early hours of the morning to get to her first job of the day on the following day. It was sad, and it pained me to see my mum suffering that way; working so hard, and more then the man who has to provide for his family but; failed by choice; preferring to sign up to the job centre for the government's money. Lelo in discomfort and loneliness, Uche talent in football a setup to be used as a tool for Malto's future financial gain, and a rude sister influencing bad manner to having bad manners sneaky and lying ways into my little brothers especially Uche, and Benjamin completely dismissed as if he never existed leaving him feeling hurt without care from his father or a proper family home. To many people including our neighbours and our relatives; Luccianna's family was a every nice, perfectly functional family; and that nothing lucked for them only because of how her father always portrayed in the outside, and also of her and hers siblings home training, education and discipline from her parents but mostly her mother. "Respect is a strong key to get on in life", says Lucianna.

She always, wanted to be close to her mum; she used to find hope, sanity, calamity, freedom of speech and to breath, and able of having a better life in her future each moment she spent and talked with her mother.

Maybe my health situation was something GOD allowed to happen to me for the glory of His name. GOD put the devil to shame then, He showed Himself to be the great I Am, the beginning and the end the Alpha and Omega. GOD allows situations to take place in our lives that we may glorify Him, he tests our faith, trust, love and believe to Him frustrating the satan, the devil and his agents.

From a; separation almost by death to having my mum as my truest friend. Julianna has become really close to her mother telling her everything about her to her mother. Once; I woke up from the intensive care at St George in Tooting; my recovery process kick started and had not stop; I grew strong and stronger as each day went by; I still live. That has only given me more assurance of His word, and of who GOD is. When He gives nobody can take away, and he had given me life, the fresh breath air for the living. What good would life be to me if I what the doctors had predicted about me came to pass? He gave me balance over my body and strengthened me.

Mother is my biggest critic, my mentor, having no one else by her to share ideas with, usually business ideas. Getting closer to my mother and learning a lot I always longed for in our relationship. Doctors had said that I would not be normal again, it was said that I would become dumb, ugly and a liability if I ever survived and live. At that moment mother had gotten weak in the body but; her faith and devotion to GOD grew bigger and deeper. Meanwhile; father was not a fully present figure but warning an unprecedented death.

Essa and Uche had told me that; Malto had even started to create a memoire area of me at his computer desk, which was at the living room, for him and possibly a funeral too. Lucinna found herself to be speechless; as she did not understand her father' actions nevertheless; she did not think so much of it since.

Looking forwards to go home before her fifteenth birthday impatiently waiting for the doctor to give her the permission for her hospital leave. I asked the ward nurses that took care of me on the regularly bases to let me go home because I thought I was fine; all my nurses were very kind and caring with me. I liked to talk to them whenever they came around in my room to check my temperature, BP, and bring my medicines. At this times mum had never left my side, and she was in the hospital premises when; she was not in my room with me, or had gone home to pick up something I might have needed. Like; more food, Cerelac was what I most ate when I was in hospital as; I could not chew so much nor swallow chunks of food down my throat. I had a lot of porridge and soup. My mother had taken time off her jobs to stay with me at the hospital; and we spent a lot of time talking though I had memory problem and I did not remember anything we spoke after we had spoken.

Mother bathed me, brushed my teeth as if I was still a baby I was weak very weak, and she fed me. I had to learn to walk all over again, as I had lost balance and strength. And; every attempts I made at walking again she saw it she was there and, excited she used to be by the gaze in her face. She was there and, she held my hand and firmly holding and supporting my arm the nurse on duty would be supporting me by holding my other arm.

Encouraging me to keep trying, making more steps forward, and holding on tight to her I used to be.

However a rapid miraculous revolution was happening in my body, I got better as each day passed by; the doctors and nurses were shocked; all exclaiming "it's a miracle. There is no way that as a human she is able to revitalise her body cells and leading her health to stability without much, stronger and major medical help other then what we have given her"; with two nurses agreeing on that. A, doctor said it was GOD's hand working in me. Well... I know for sure it was GOD reconnecting my thread of life for a purpose. Few days before miraculous changes were happening in my body the doctors were saying otherwise

'There is nothing else they could do, they have tried, and waiting for me to die and; if didn't'

The nurses feeling sorry for me, and they did not see or believe to be a reason for hope... I was dead, before I died in their eyes but; not GOD! Jesus said 'I came to give life and life more then abundant', He did not lie, and GOD did not fail my cause.

My maternal relatives were always at the doorstep of the hospital visiting me and, being of strength to my mother; they also called every time for news of how I was getting on as days passed by. My grandmother who is in Africa called the hospital every day to speak to my mother... and enquired about me and my health but; never once I felt, saw, knew or heard of the presence of my paternal relatives. Not to talk of my father's presence, and wanting to be praise at the aftermath for the prayers he made for me and managing to get out of bed to visit me at the hospital; a matter I care not to look back onto. Life goes on... though many times I wanted to ask him questions, but knowing the person he is, asking questions would be a waste of time, and the beginning of World War III. The more I was convinced of that through his actions towards Lelo the closer I got to my mother; Lucianna has always been a good observer.

I promised GOD that I would always be strong and seek His will first. When; I left the hospital. I was determined not to fall into any youth culture by mistake, as I always knew not to be involved with such. I wanted not to walk, dress, speak, and look like them. All I wanted was to be closer and faithful to GOD; one day I thought to myself 'I will do right by GOD, and by 'being close to mum, I will learn a lot, how to live, how to care, cook, and have some positive and strong

A Mural of Till Gate Part
Made in-2010
Made with-Acrylic paint

This; painting Lucianna made for her A Level Applied Art & Design final project; the painting was later lost according to a teacher in the art department; or stolen in the possession college. Lucianna stared at this painting and always remember what the doctors had said about her; "'she will never be able to do what she loves" '; art and design has always been Luciana's love, an endless love for five art. She was well pleased with her handwork.

ground foundations'; which was something many young girls around that time seemed to run from and swapping with a tong boy, street life, bad girl behaviour, tough girl lifestyle. Many of these girls, used to go as far stealing every day from shops whether it was stealing clothes, school uniform, shoes, snacks at the grocery supermarket stores... they all did it.

There was a fashion called 'underage pregnancy'; underage pregnancy was a very high fashion, especially for the may disadvantaged young girls, girls who came from broken homes, who often did not have a good relationship with their mothers at home or did not have a father nor known their fathers while growing up at all. They; urged to find a father figure by having a boyfriend after a boyfriend, sleeping around, doing all sorts of things for attention including having sex in public.

There were; a lot of story going around town of certain girls having sex and also loosing their virginity in the bushes; at the park, in plain day light, whilst other people were also using the park as a place of attraction and calamity, peace and social enjoyments. I used to be disgusted listening to those stories. I didn't and never had met any of the girls whom I heard did engaged in the sexual activities in the park or any other public places as; the bus, somebody garden fence... I might have known one or two people; one was the girlfriend of a young man who at the time was a top little boy in the street lifestyle. He belonged to a very dangerous crew; he was dangerous! And, the other girl was just a crowd follower who strived for more and more attention and fame leaving her mark of a bad and top girl who had her first time sexual intercourse with her Somali boyfriend at Wandow Park. I had heard by the mass youth in the streets, and even my friends at school also told me it. But I also knew it was possible that those things were happening; everything had changed and South London, the town became heavily marginalised, young fourteen years old teenagers had become wild! And behaved as though they were twenty-five to thirty years old adults, with the underage pregnancy rate at its highest point each year in south London. I did not doubt the truth. I did not want to fall into that category of teenager who closed their minds and heart and their salvation, future and destiny which GOD had traced for them by trading their star for a here and now amusement, treating and looking at the things of GOD as a joke. I did not know what it was to live that lifestyle but; I ask myself what was the goal in hurting themselves?

'GOD had taken me from a place; saving my life over and over', when I left the hospital, I left it with a straightforward mindset; I knew what I wanted and needed to do and, so that was the one path mother had always taught me in 'GOD's path'.

Lucianna looks back at when she finally discovered, and started to understand that GOD had a plan for her life, and that she is to serve a purpose one which; she was also able to confirm months after, starting school again.

She was told she would never be the same

Being different from everybody else; never to be pretty not even with a smile on her face she was going to be pretty

Lucianna heard, her mother heard, her father heard; they heard she will be talentless, and a bum

'She will be a ugly person'; they said; Lucianna wonders if what and how she looks like today is what her meningitis doctors said she would look like if she survived meningitis and lived.

Science has its prediction by facts about the human nature and body through what the particles that make up the human body cell Created by GOD through; the characteristics of these particles predictions are foreseen and set up by scientists assumed to be correct by health care constitution around the world. Feared by the peoples, pulling lives apart in advance of any diagnosed illness and diseases effect to ones body. But; one thing scientists fell to acknowledge is that; GOD is the Master of science and the Provider of all scientific knowledge, wisdom and intelligence, only GOD can undo what He has done and what He had written, and nothing can erase it; He is a healer and a provider to the need. Circumstances change, the world is constantly changing, but; His word, will, grace, and mercy never change. The Bible says that 'Heaven and Earth shall pass away but His word will remain'; science and technology it's being revolutionised at all time, just as for every one second, one point seventy-eight people die. Lucianna believes that; it was the word. The will, the grace and, the love of GOD that kept her alive; it had resurrected her from within the deepest of her... Her soul.

I never took my mind off Jesus, I did not; when mother sang worship and praises to GOD whilst she was seeking GOD's face and I, being unconscious joined mother in worship and praise in the name of Jesus.

Mother was very happy, and joyous! That was a sign that He had been hearing her prayers, her cries, her supplications and He had also taken to account all the services I had rendered to GOD before my falling ill with TB meningitis.

The six o'clock in the morning evangelism, voluntarily cleaning the church, spend all my time reading and striving to understand His word, seeking his face after midnight in the night early hours of the morning, and praying for the youths of my generation, young people like; me, Lelo, Tamy, troubled with problems at home, school and, lost etc. but, that I had never met, and I will probably also never meet in my life. Just, know that I prayed and fasted for my whole generation of South London, London, England. Remembering back then I took what I was doing for GOD as not so much that; He would remember or, could remember me for... but mother always tells me

"In your time of trouble, distress and desperation, when you pray, remind GOD... remind him of all the things you did for Him, God sees all these thing, because you, remind Him in your prayers He will move for you."

I was belittled most of the times that; I did something at church in the house of GOD for GOD;
Belittled for trying to do the things I was not costumed to doing, and
For being different; the youths looked at me and searched in their minds and likeness of the type of group of young people I fitted in best. Failing to acknowledge that; just as I was different in their eyes and mind, I was also doing the things I did in the church for GOD; which were the things they did not see to be out of love for GOD.

When I did it right without repetition I was instantly screwed. And I received a wave of under breath insults by no other then the same person who had claimed to be my best friend; Tamy especially. It was either I stayed at the same level as her, or I be less then her but; never should I be better then her in any circumstance excluding our individual professional talents and skills. Her sister; Temirah was never allowed to match her, or look better then her, since she was a tongue boy and, Tamy was used to being ashamed of her sister maybe she thought that;

if her sister looked like her or better then her it would have made the competition hard for her... it's how she made it seem and their relationship as sisters.

Lucianna did not feel so welcomed in the beginning when she started attending the church youth group services after the Sundays' church service, but Lucianna did not think much of it "neither was I looking for friends at that church"; says Lucianna; as she was used to not having many friend before, and thought of the people there of being delinquent juveniles.

I was well, I went to church because, that is what I believed in from ever since; Jesus Christ, and when I went to church I went to worship GOD so; I also did not feel like I needed or wanted friends. However; the only reason I went to that church was because; my dad forced the family to go to that church, his niece who I, my siblings and my mother had never met and never had ever made an effort to step into our house in my country to visit her much younger cousins before came to our house in Friars Wood. Portraying to being a saint; in the forefront; but a liar, loud and perverted as; she caused things to be at home for us... I felt and still feel that; she knew what she was doing. But; she also seemed satisfied that se did and acted the way she did, taking the place of a daughter and more important then the children owners of the house. Forgetting her place; she was a stranger the only person who knew her and knew and had both spent time together was my father.

In the middle of a very disorganised bunch of young people, who lived their lives for the moment and not for GOD as they so exclaimed I did not want to be identified with them although; I also, practiced acceptance, forgiving, and coexistence with them. Jesus said many will say, "Lord Lord, I prophesied in Your name, I have cast out demons in Your name", and Jesus will tell them "Depart from me for I do not know you"; these are the words that many Christians have heard and read from their Holy Bible, at first hand but; the ironic thing is that many of them fail to live up to what is expected of them as children of GOD by GOD except; from they are really not. Not by the society and what the media condemns or not, but by the word of God. While; some take the Holy Bible to be just mare words with no power to impact their lives if they believe in GOD in the name of Jesus or, not.

Especially the young people, there is a tendency of following the crowd, what their friends and how the friend of their friend lives like that draws the two friend so close making you the odd one out. Many Christians including pastors, protocols, pastors' wives especially; also fail to acknowledge while up in their ministries that the Holy Bible represents faith in GOD, and is the word of GOD. Jesus came to earth through the natural human childbirth canal, and He carried the burdens of the unbeliever and of the believer, and our sins, and He died for us on the cross. He rose again on the third day and appeared to His disciples without wounds on His flesh; except from the holes by the nails on the cross of Calvary, and in clean garment cleaner then those who had a bath or shower on the day Jesus appeared to the disciples. Around five hundred people witnessed Jesus alive after He was put in His grave. The sinners were not crucified for their sins, iniquities and transgressions. Amongst the five hundred people who saw Jesus there were people who were not disciples, nor follower and worshipers making them witnesses, and many who then believed. Jesus departed back to where He was sent from GOD the Father in Heaven, whom from we were all made and spoken to existence. The hope, that on earth you can have a better life and your tears you will wipe away; hope is faith.

Once I started to hang out with the youth group after the youth services on Sundays outside the church, I became realistic to the truth about whom they really were. I could not understand how a group of young people who met at church and would act like saints in the church though still displaying a human imperfection attitude and character; which is normal as a human. But; were totally the opposite outside the church.

It was fun to be at home with the family but only if mother and Lelo were there especially the days of late after my hospital leave, mother and I became inseparable, whilst my father and I drifted apart. I had found strength being apart from the youth group whilst; I was in the hospital, and I felt as if GOD had given me strength to overcome the many more fights of my life. But at the same time; I felt as though I had found myself without spiritual assistance and guidance however; never alone!

I saw how; most young girls were with their mothers, and that strengthened me to look for a better relationship with my own mother. I saw that their relationship with their mother was far worst then of mine and mine mother and; their lives also dragged to the mad by themselves because of their own choices. I was a good observer from childhood, and I did not want my relationship with my mother to ever get to the same level as many of those young girls I met at the youth group, school, and saw out there. I had also; found strength to stand up to my dad for the many wrong things he used to do and still does to the family I stood up to him by allowing the distance to take place between us. I became vocal and opinionated even though I had always been. But; this time around it was different because; I was serious, I was tired of the terrorism, and intimidations to agree and go along with everything he said just because he is the man of the house; in his mind. The more I wanted to be closer to mother, the more I was closer to mother the more I wanted her to have only the best in life and be happy for the rest of her entire life. It was painfully hard to have watched Julianna go through the many things she went through in her marriage to Malto my dad; I have never seen happiness for my mother with my father. To make it worse; there's a specific relative who comes around and; when they do they made things only worst for my mother. Adding; pressure, headaches of her own personal problems; of her marriage, family and social life too, she immensely disrespected my mother even in our home. Her assignment seemed to be; to divert my father's mind into perversion ways of adultery once again, after all the infidelities mothers had gone through and; she knew of some of them; but she delighted in seeing her sister my mother humiliated, sad, stressed, unhappy, worried, ashamed and embarrassed. Some family members are worst then your bad friend, but a friend that does not help you in the way of GOD whether they believe or not, is also not a good friend, but they might not think so, as by the obvious. Especially; those who do know the truth however; for those who do not know the truth they fail to come to term with the truth because; of their choice in life, and their negligence soon becomes ignorance, altogether.

Reversed Psychology

Four; days later Lelo was taken to custody, that boy was arrested, we did not and still do not know his arrest came about, and how the police found him. The boy knew heard of Lelo's arrest on the same night that the incident caused by that boy happened; which was the day after he was seen with the pink knife in college, and he went in hiding, that only his family knew where he was. Whether they knew what; or where he was or not, was a mystery. As everything about them is a mystery; in frustrating themselves into other people's live and how they live to spoil it, and then they disappear after spoiling it; acting all innocent and victimized meanwhile; it is their plan all along. 'Children of satan they are'; they seem to live for the motif to steal, kill, and destroy. My brother's life was a their evil and satanic project, but is impossible that they took that task this far without any internal help from within the four corners of the house we where in; the family. Sometimes; I thought that Malto and his daughter have a full on hand in all the negative things that has taken place in our lives; in the life of me, Lelo, Uche, and Benjamin. But; however it has all been confirmed. 'Woe to him and her who plans and do wickedness against the children of GOD'; with Malto and, for the most part of his family.

A; legal team for Lelo twice at different time, and we know that; the job of a solicitor and lawyer is to lie; but lie to get the client in a better position of the situation. Lelo found himself unlucky with both solicitors; information about his case were being communicated and passed over to the other side, including his statement to that other boy and his legal team. Evidently; he boy and his family wanted to destroy and take Lelo down, from the beginning, by stealing another person's innocence after stealing away a human life 'was carrying the knife and revealed possession of it at the Dingwall Road bus stop.'; that was a lie, Lelo had never carried a knife or, hurt anybody, they wanted him to be Lelo, but they felt because, the truth will always be the truth, and innocence can not be bought, and what is hidden in the dark always come to light. Both, of Lelos' solicitor knew, knew and had concrete evidences that that boy carried a knife, and also used it early that morning. A tall clown of a man, dark skin colour, he was Tamil, Asian saw the desperation Julianna had and the faith in GOD that her family had for Lelos' vindication in his court case, and took advantage. His second solicitor at Lloyd's a corrupt and a hypocrite man without integrity, the things he did to Julianna's boy case showed how degraded that man was, and probably still is. We later found out that the things he did in Lelos' case he had also done to others many young people in exchange of money "Your family has no connections"; he once told when; he was telling me that; there was not much time, and that the court trials starting date was very close, and that my brother would not had been in this case if; we had contacted him from the beginning, but we knew not him. And, he also took advantage; he blind-sided Lelo, and the family. After he messed up, he started to run away... Not answering our phone calls, not replying emails, it was a huge gang of professionals and non-professionals including that boy and his family who were after to destroy Lelo, trying to sell his life to the devil for money; what a good for nothing hard work! Well the professionals did not care because at the end of the day they received their salary. I hope they have never been able to go asleep at night, and felt like murderers, but compassion I know they do not feel. They did not undo what they did against Lelo, and diverted the cause of justice, they even stole his fund so that would seem to be the reason why solicitors would not want to work on his case due to no fund of appeal.

I remember once after the sentencing my parents and I were looking to meet and speak to the Tamil solicitor to find out about what had happened to the case, why was the outcome what it was, and why was he not in court in the last few days of the trial and the sentencing day, but all attempts felled to no avail.

There, was no reply, response, answer or reaction from that man. Many, times I sent him a text message I asked him about the case of appeal for my brother, after he had promised me many times, as we as mother during phone calls and face to face discussion of the possibilities of the appeal for Lelo and he told me that he was going to call me later to talk about, that he busy, but he never again called or picked up my phone calls or calls from anyone else from my family. And, after one month or two I received a text message from his colleague another tall solicitor telling me that the solicitor told him to text me, to let me know that they have the application for an appeal for Lelo had been made, and I texted him back and asked them how is that and when? This man has not been in communication with even Lelo, nor us so how was the application put through, and if so why has not gotten in touch with my father. As, Malto did a good job fooling himself pretending to care about the case, as a father to receive information, to then talk bad about Lelo and curse him. My mother used to tell him everything, I strongly disagreed with that, and so everything I knew, what I had found out about his case to help, or thought I never discussed with him. He was not Lelo's he was his enemy who was happy with what was happening with Lelo. Lelo was seventeen when it first happened, and eighteen at the time of the trials, and heavenly persecuted by everybody including his father, it was no a surprise to Lucianna that Malto took pleasure in it. But that solicitor the colleague, never replied. He knew that; I knew that; corruption was going on...

In The House

I saw these things happening and my father embarrassed them. When my auntie came back from France claiming to want to visit us for holidays, whilst mother was filled with problems that had filled her mind, needing support and assistance from her family, but the closest to mother was her sister and the same person who has always held the worst interest at heart for my mother. The sister who drove her husband's name to the mad insulting him insulting my mother insulting our family causing stirs between husband and wife and other families too like; a demon sent from hell to cause separation, and divorce of family. She used to come to our home for her so called 'visit to the family'; walk around the house almost naked around my father whenever; my mother was not in her exact location inside the house to see her sexually arousing and performing sexual erotic advances towards Malto. All this happened whilst; I was there, seeing it all, and her toddler children craving for her attention and my toddler siblings running around the house past her and my father up and down the stairs; in and out of their bedroom where Lina her name, happened to sleep in every time she came to sleep over or for her actual sexual advances towards my father holidays and insulting behaviour and disrespect towards my mother. She was either in our bathroom using the toilet with the door wide open as if she was sharing the house with her husband and her children alone. She then stood wearing her African pan purposely mal wrapped around her waist falling down to her hips, many times showing her crack, her buttocks,

147

but; at all times she flaunted her body, her buttocks and the top parts of her body especially to my father on her attendance in our house, while my mother would be in the kitchen cooking, or cleaning the downstairs part of the house, including feeding her sister's own children. Mean while her sister was flirting with her husband and by what I witnessed with my eyes she also; sexually provoked him, and trying to bad mouth her to me. She was always mal dressed showed her under wears whenever; she brought herself around my dad she made sure to wear a string and flash it out in his face. 'Her sister's husband, in her sister's house in the moment her sister was down on the floor and was not following where about she was and was doing in her house'; she humiliated my mum in front of me as though she was making a point to send a message out to my mother, and took advantage of her kindness. How disrespectful and disgusting. The only message I could see through my auntie's actions and behaviour was;

'Not a role model, jealousy, hatred, envy, undisciplined, family disoriented, not worthy of sisterhood, home wrecker, filthy and a 'ndumba' of the fifth category'; the words I wish to speak out loud, every time I see her.

My father once referred to her as a ndumba (prostitute) I guess he has his own reasons for it at first hand! But; I never found the difference between the two of them... including the occult practices Malto does at home, he thinks that he can trick us into selling our souls to the devil, like he did to his soul. Hiding; it, and used the word of GOD as a masquerade for his juju, lately he invited his cousin from his birth place to spend Christmas with us, bringing along his witchcraft, they planned to conduct a satanic ritual in our house trying to subject mother and I along with Lelo, Uche and Benjamin into accepting his false GOD, the one that he worship that is not the true and living GOD of Israel. They are both the same with no shame.

I often ran down the stairs to my mother to tell her what was happening, but mother always acted as if I was wrong, and saw things the wrong way. And I always asked her 'How?' I was there, I saw and heard the things she did and said. At times she used to say things; that were very insulting to my mother intentionally and, directly to my face; behind my mothers back, giving me the impression that she hoped to influence me against my mother, and teaching me to hate my own mum as she hated, and despised hers. Oh well! At least today I know that those were her true intentions and I know why too... "You call your mother, but you do not call me!"; one day she told me that; when she was talking to me what it seemed like she expects me to stop my life for her, and take her as my mother instead of my mother.

"How dare she comparing herself to my mother and try to condemn my relationship with my mother, is she crazy? She has children of her own why does she thinks that it is okay; that I give my daughterly attention to her instead of my own mother? "You call your mother but; you do not call me!""; I angrily wanted to burst that out on her at that very moment; but I controlled myself, and told my brothers who; after hearing of it; became angered. 'She better find her line'; was the expression Benjamin, Uche and Lelo gave me in respond to the many things she has always done "She is my mother. Are; you mother?"; I asked her, and the back and forth continued to her telling me that she is also my mother just because; she is my mother's sister and therefore; she deserves equal if not better treatment then mother, and I reinsuring her that; my mother will always be my mother. Besides; Lucianna thinks that; the value of mother is not given to every women who is not her mother apart; from her birth mother, and there are three women that I do consider and call mother, because they do give themselves such value, respect, GOD fearing woman, and they are also positive role models to Lucianna, as well as; they are mothers too.

I was mad at my father for never telling her off, and showing her that that was a family house and a family which; belongs to mother and him at that. That; the home and marriage of my parents is secrete; since he so believes to be a righteous man, and GOD's only instrument of the family. I wanted him to stand up for his wife my mother and let shame fill that other women's face mother's sister. I felt disrespected that my mother was disrespect in front of me and behind her back by her own so called sister. Resentment towards my father and Lina, and I will never accept them to take part in my live as a relative, but I believe that GOD is the most righteous judge. Mother tells me all the time; especially when I make remarks about what people do against people for example:

In the case of Lina on my mother today; people of same nations depart to fight one another, and torn apart.

She tells me; don't worry yourself, "what's done and said here on earth is also paid here on earth before death"; she says this in the most calm voice with assurance that one day those who had hurt her or others whether she knows or not will be repaid back with the same portion of pain they have caused her or others. And she is right! GOD is a just GOD, why should one worry and fear the evil's doing of others, when GOD is the supreme judge of all judges, and we have the greatest attorney in Jesus?

As long as Jesus is Lord you shall not fear evil, for they have no authority over your life, and GOD has the final say over our lives.

2 Corinthians 5:10

'Or we must all appear before the judgement seat of Christ, that each one may receive the things done in the body, according to what he has done, whether good or bad.'

The word of GOD never lies, for GOD is neither a man that He should lie nor a son of man that He should deceive.

Untie Lina, got married to a man whom soon after he paid her bride price she gave birth to her first child, and then decided to move to France with her husband who; also soon showed the true colours of their marriage, and his truest colours.

Whilst she had taken upon herself to go from household to household to find and take information for destruction; planning and devising and opening her foul mouth wide open to lie, gossip and make rumours about one house to the other from; one individual to the next. In her own household a lot was happening, her husband dumped her, he would kick her out of his house and she would shelter herself in the tube stations of Paris how ironic! Lina is the woman that goes about others household leaving every marriage and couples in trouble who she found peace on her arrival; and insulted others, her sister and cousins relationships, husbands and spoke of how her husband is better then others. Meanwhile; she was getting beaten and yelled at everyday by her husband or former husband behind closed doors.

A men of sixties years of age almost seventy and out of embarrassment she lied to everyone that he was the same age as her fake age.

The whole family was stunted, at the appearance of her ex and husband; of an old man, very tall, and skinny as a pipeline tube, looking physically, mentally weak.

I remember my other unties used to talk about it in desolation. How sad, that she fell pregnant for such man. Prayerful shades were being thrown around "'Yaya (Big sister), we have to pray hard so that that baby she is carrying in her belly will look like our side of the family'"; one of my untie told my mother that on the phone once... he is a very ugly man.

Lelo and I, who were young children of eleven and twelve years of age, knew that her husband was old. We used to laugh, and giggle about it, and we could tell that; they portrayed about their marriage and relationship was a façade. We thought he was really old and very ugly.

Whenever; he came to our house, he ported himself as, though he was a very important person, his posture said a lot, but nothing to do with intelligence or a high class of living. He portrayed a 'wanna be' and 'make believe' lifestyle.

Nevertheless; unlike her, her lifestyle and the marriage she had was never our fixation. We cared not about how her married life was like; as long as she was happy as she very often portrayed to be, and made him look so important, as if he was the man of centuries. But; in the end she paid for the much wickedness she did to others before and during her marriage. She had forgotten that she was a woman, and that GOD sees answers the cry of just cause of every women. She did not fear GOD, meanwhile the word of GOD applies to everyone, and we are all the same to GOD. When you persecute your brother endlessly, it is the vengeance of GOD that you will meet with.

'For we must all appear before the judgement seat of Christ, that each one may receive the things done in the body, according to what he has done, whether good or bad.' 2 Corinthians 5:10

When my mother, my siblings and I where living in Paris; there were rumours that Lina dated my father, knowing that it is her sister's husband. Other; rumours were that they had had physical sexual relationship... I remember when I used to hear these things I used to feel angry, I did not know what to think of my dad or of my auntie and now, whenever she comes around since before her marriage to the tall man; she has always flaunted her body and exposed it in front of Malto to him specifically. I believed the rumours and more, they had or maybe still had a spiritual satanic tie, and guess against who? It is pretty obvious. A huge disrespect, she has no notion of boundaries. In those moments I wished I could scream at her, yell in her face, and call her to her face according to the behaviour she displayed. But, I held back, I held back and told my mother of the things I had seen and witnessed, you know... Her sister's behave and her husband's silence response of acceptance to the availability in display. Is; what I saw and understood. However she never believed me, and she made excuses for her sister's behaviour, as if I was blind and did not see right as always; mother second guessed my opinion and evident facts I presented to her on any matter. Most of the time it seemed like all that was left for her to tell me was that 'I did not see it'; therefore as some wealthy people say 'not guilty till proven guilty', but I was the witness with the evidences, and yet she ignored me. Her only phrase was; 'what is done on earth is paid on earth before the person dies'.

Julianna still did not say nor do anything, but Lucianna recognises that; she waited for GOD's judgement. She; trusts His judgement but for the most is because; Julianna generally hardly paid attention to anything Lucianna told her, but Lucianna never disregarded her mother and her teachings to Lucianna.

"'Through wisdom is an house build; and by understanding it is established'" Proverbs 24:3

Surely my mother was preparing and training me to love and patience. Lucianna never lied, from hers very early age, and just like most parent teach and train their children to do good, and that to lie is wrong and is a sin. In most Christian household, and non-believing household, she believes

"At least when I was growing up, the Christian Bible believing faith family my mum knew, and the children I mostly played with, when I played with others then my siblings were brought with the fear of GOD. It is GOD's commandment that we shall not lie nor bare false witness against our neighbours."

Though; I have lied in the past about minor things, yes but; a lie is a lie. No matter how big or small it is. But; never would

I have lied about such things, No way! These are very serious allegations, unless I witnessed them, which I did witnessed it and I found the things I had seen to be wrong. Most of the lies Lucianna told were said as a joke, when she was joking and with her siblings, and she made up stories, and they would giggle at them, then say to Lucianna 'that was a lie'; and she would laugh along once more, as she enjoyed a fun laughing time with her siblings though they knew it was not a real life story, it was just a joke for the moment. Nothing harmful and disappointing was ever uttered. Moments like those, she felt most loved and little peace, as long as Malto was not around to see the union and love amongst the sibling, because; when Malto was around there was fun time. Her jokes; could make others laugh and loosen up, although there was always a spoiler, when one of her siblings would come up with a better and funnier joke, which made them including their mother laugh; harder then what her jokes did, that always used to be Lelo's jokes. Most of them were to pick at Lucianna. "Oy! Baby elephant"; he used to say in the break of his jokes... But never once was there jealousy in the midst of the four siblings. It was always a time of happiness, also tears and rage for Lucianna at times when Lelo took over with his jokes because; he would also picked on her.

"Real brother and sisterhood times we used to have"; as Lucianna calls it at the remembrance, the jokes and rages from arguments and sometimes fights she used to have with Lelo that never lasted for more then five to ten minutes.

Lucianna believes that as; her mother heard, and listened to her repeated complains and telling of the awful thing Lucianna had witnessed and had mentally endured as a child from her untie and father's behaviour, and Julianna never uttered confrontation against either of the two adults; in the wisdom of GOD, GOD ordered his punishment on Lina through what; she had surpassed in her marriage to the tall man. Her mother's children amidst of persecutions, and evil minded behaviour and plans of her father, to always cause division and negligence among the children and mother and to divert all attention to him as the 'dictator', and do as he orders. Her and her siblings and her mother have only grown closer united, with more love and care for each other.

Love has been established in our house among us the children, because my mother chose to be wise.

Her way of protection to us, incomprehensible to us sometimes especially me, but GOD has a plan, our patience and union is needed with total focus on Him.

"'Blessed is that man that maketh the LORD his trust, and respecteth not the proud, nor such as turn aside to lies.'" Psalm 40:4

Because of her trust in GOD and fear of GOD, GOD answered my mother's enemy from afar off places and the enemies who are up close including her sister.

And like the Bible says;

"'He who says he is in the light, and hates his brother, is in the darkness until now'" The First Epistle of John 2:9

To know, accept and to live in the Lord Jesus Christ, is to live in the countenance of truth, be in the light, saved and is to know love. To truly love is to be set free. If, Lina was free indeed; arousing her sister's and other people's life wouldn't be her business and worry.

"He who does not love does not know GOD, for GOD is love'"; Says The First Epistle John 4:8

Love has held Lucianna together, and closer to GOD, and it GOD's love even when there are evildoers among in between and trying to cause gaps and creating holes.

Who; prepared and dag pits which; came in different forms all throughout her life against us; my mum my brothers and, me; the love of Jesus and in Jesus Christ GOD has protected us, for is the love of GOD, I believe and trust.

The journey; does not and has not ended here. In every a bad situation of my life good and grace His praise had came out of it to Him Elohim, because GOD wanted me and allowed me to know Him, His works and the difference between those who serve him and those who do not. Many; so called pastors in Europe and America are not even pastors; they do services in their churches saying in the name of Jesus when indeed; their hearts and mind they intend evil, they are used by satan; by their own choices, and all that they want and destroy your life for is money and, world power domination. They are everywhere; antichrists; on television worship channels, their books. I bare in mind and we should all know, that there are also some pastors and churches of GOD, the Lord Jesus Christ undefiled; who are devoted to GOD and His will, who GOD uses for the deliverance of his people. He uses man and women, the youths and the children too. It has only just occurred me that; I cannot be mad at any bad situation, myself, and especially GOD! I must trust Him always, allowing my head, soul, mind, body, heart, bones, and my thoughts extol Him Yahweh, Jehovah Jireh, Jehovah Shama the Elohim. He is the beginning and, the end the Alpha and Omega; the GOD of Israel. Deliverance, freedom, faith, strength, love and grace come from him.

Lucianna feels that GOD has been watching her, her life since her beginning 'that is why He is always there... Jesus is alive and he intercedes' for me day and night'; every time Lucianna thinks of His goodness she is humbled within herself.

Although I cannot be angry I do, because is my right of expression towards GOD in regard of my situation, troubles and trials, and then comes the frustration, but is what to be avoided, because it is GOD who is to be the first and the last word. Life is complicated, however when you invite GOD into your play, He will make your life beautiful. Avoid; destructions for they are; from the devil, be wise, and search for GOD and understanding. Find; GOD in his scriptures fear GOD and Love Jesus Christ, it is free to love, love indeed and love one another.

When somebody loves something or somebody, he or she will protect, and not hurt is an affiliation of hate, the word love is not heard or understood, and felt with words only or a metaphysical emotion that; is so called chemistry, and it is not sex; true love isn't sex nor found in sexual relationship between a man or a women and certainly between the same sex. Love is clear when ones word is backed by actions.

When is always, or slightly to be a lie in the things that matter in life, is neither love, or out of love, and it is to be selfishness you lie to hide what you did, say, or said, planed, and the wrong, mistake, and the cheat is hidden by the lies. Most people who are two faced, cheaters and liars; displaying a false image of the reality of their lives whilst; also pretending to be someone, soothing that they are not. Faking individual character and even personality but; it only takes a close insight appearance and look to know the truth of ones life and way of living, on the other hand, for the person who purposely do such, and lives in the other person's life only to see the proves of its reality, puts him, or herself in the position of self denial of love. It; mostly happens out of envy, and the thoughts to do something as so; to another individual begins out of, and it is generated and fed by envy, jealousy, impurity, and curiosity which creates the beginning of a malicious circle enclosed in evilness.

The; epidemic of the opposite of love is envy the nature of jealousy and hatred and; the door opener for malice. Malice is something that; some do it directly and do not hide what they have done by simply not talking about it, is something done in the dark, other first plot with the expectation of the plot to unravel itself into a bomb which; causes a huge bomb of distraction in somebody's life in a matter of lifetime frame. If it's not a good seed from a good a positive source; if it is not from GOD, it is a satanic work, for GOD is light not darkness, and His plans are of goodness and works are beautiful. They; of peace joy, happiness and love of everlasting, and no works on this planet and they entire universe can compare to GOD's work. The, sole creator of the universe although; many think that the universe created itself, and known as the 'big bang'; however if big bang created our universe who then; made big bang, and all that energy.

When; the Jews wanted to stone the women caught committing adultery; before they did, and tried to do so, something that would had killed the women they took her to Jesus, with the intention to test Him in the condemnation of the women. But; before Jesus even spoke each one of the man who were present with their evil intention; became also, confused, convicted, by their conscience.

"'I am the light of the world. He who follows Me shall not walk in darkness, but have the light of life.'"; Says Jesus Christ book of John 8:12.

This is thee maker; the great I am GOD created this universe, and He gave the power of love to us allowing us to choose what we decide to take and believe. The universe did not make itself or any human being. To love yourself; is accept yourself and to accept yourself is to, accept where we come from, and where come from, is found in the ancient of days, before the time began, we came from a maker, we came from GOD. Love is pure, GOD is pure, and He is seven times holy;

GOD in His throne, authority and wisdom; which He also gave to us individually; that by His word He created everything and by His power which; He has also given us which; lays in our tongue so that, we can destroy evil and be set free "'He who is without sin, let him throw a stone first.'"; the Jewish man wanted for Jesus to say throw a stone and kill her because she is an adulterer because; they did not accept Jesus nor believed that He was the Son of GOD, there to redeem them and, everybody. They, also came to Jesus with evil intention, but Jesus stood up, and told them who are you to judge, and the evil was destroyed and neutralised by the. To love is to take care of yourself first then others, your neighbour '"Beloved, do not estimate what is evil, but what is good. He who does good is of GOD, but he who does evil has not seen GOD"'; be positive although; life may come against you, and you might grow fears of attacks. Why do you fear? When GOD is alive and Christ Jesus is the attorney, if you allow him to be yours; He will take you case in his hand.

True love is to be humble at heart and strong in the spirit; and do not mistake humbleness to shame; you will be in shame because; you have not been humble.

Because you love; the love from the highest throne above the circle of the world will descends upon your life. "The lover one is a GOD blessed creature..." ; Says Lucianna.

> To Love is to obtain the most powerful
> weapon in the universe.
>
> A universal language that is discovered as,
> time goes on. Because; life is a teacher!

'If you are reproached for the name of
Christ, blessed are you, for the Spirit of
glory and of God rests upon you.'

Peter 4:12

And; in the midst of all stands Malto and his daughter Essa; they do not want to stop their dark ways; casting evil looks, curses, on spiritual and physical spiritually battles, at day, afternoons and night times against; me and my family. Malto wants to continue with his jujus, satanic and cultism practices along with the black magic; ready at the order of his other half evil centric daughter Essa, to kill, destroy and steal and his anger at the pursuit of power and wealth at the expense and blessings GOD commanded from before time began for my brothers, mother and I. The devil himself knows that it's a mission impossible... "Looses they are"; says Lucianna.

"Voce es uma mã mulher se casamos, emvez de esceitar e rezar no dues da minha familhia reza; taz a rezar este DEUS (We married and instead of you accepting and praying to the god of my family; you are praying to this GOD, you are a bad wife)"; he told julianna, with a voice of regret, and tiredness of trying to turn my mother into a witch, I and my brothers, and not being able to accomplish his and his fathers' satan's plan.

"Qual é ou Deus da tua familhia, eu conheço Jesus Christo, ou senhor dos senhores, esse é ou DEUS; antes da gente se casar na Russia não acordamos que vamos seguir e servire so ou uniquo DEUS Jesus Christo? (What is the god of your family, I only know Jesus Christ the Lord of Lords He is GOD; before we got married in Russia did we not agree that; we will follow and serve only the only GOD Jesus Christ?)"; Julianna replied Malto, and from his silence she understood that; that man was up to dark things and worships satan 'the god of his family there in the village of Cabinda' 'mmmm feitiço deles, as practices e sensos oculto I will never follow nor be part of any of it'. Jesus Christ has already paid the price; and the devil has not room for him. Malto's family god is not accepted and never will, for he is not the GOD of Israel, Abraham Isaac and Jacob.

The world is damaged and dominated by dark powers in your houses, schools, colleges, works places, the clothes we wear, the shoes we wear, and in the food we eat; Jesus Christ of Nazareth is the only way, GOD is available for anyone who wants Him, and salvation is at hand, and the kingdom of GOD is taken by force therefore; we must also watch and pray for our own good.

I remember once I asked an auntie of mine in my mother's side of the family about; the handbags her husband was selling, and if he was still selling them, because I wanted to buy a designer's bag from him, and I also wanted to know the price. Unfortunately; he no longer sold designers handbags for women however; she one day called me to tell me that she had a handbag for me, that she had bought on holiday in the united states of America, and that she just; thought of giving it to me. I said it is okay auntie, not thank you, but she insisted that I had that handbag... Eventually I accepted her offer and said thank you, and weeks later I went to her house to pick up the handbag and visit her and my cousin. On that night whilst I was sleeping laying on my bed; I saw her, and she screamed my name loud, as of she called my name, I saw her in my sleep, and I did not answer her, instead I got up and I prayed to GOD my deliverer, and never again I saw her in the same way at night, and in my sleep. I was chocked at the attempt, but GOD used to also show me who is truly who and stand affirmed with my 'No'. Appearance; smiles, kindnesses and they word family are deceiving; the fight is not seen in the flesh.

Printed in the United States
by Baker & Taylor Publisher Services